Simple & Natural
SOAPMAKING

CREATE 100% PURE AND BEAUTIFUL SOAPS WITH
THE NERDY FARM WIFE'S EASY RECIPES AND TECHNIQUES

Jan Berry

AUTHOR OF *101 EASY HOMEMADE PRODUCTS FOR YOUR SKIN,
HEALTH & HOME* AND FOUNDER OF THE NERDY FARM WIFE

PAGE STREET
PUBLISHING CO.

PAGE STREET
PUBLISHING CO.

First published in 2017 by

Page Street Publishing Co.

27 Congress Street, Suite 105

Salem, MA 01970

www.pagestreetpublishing.com

Distributed by Macmillan, sales in Canada by The Canadian Manda Group.

23 22 21 20   6 7

ISBN-13: 978-1-62414-384-7

ISBN-10: 1-62414-384-9

Library of Congress Control Number: 2017932887

Cover and book design by Page Street Publishing Co.

Photography by Jan Berry, except photo of soap separation on page 183 by Andrea Satterthwaite

Printed and bound in China

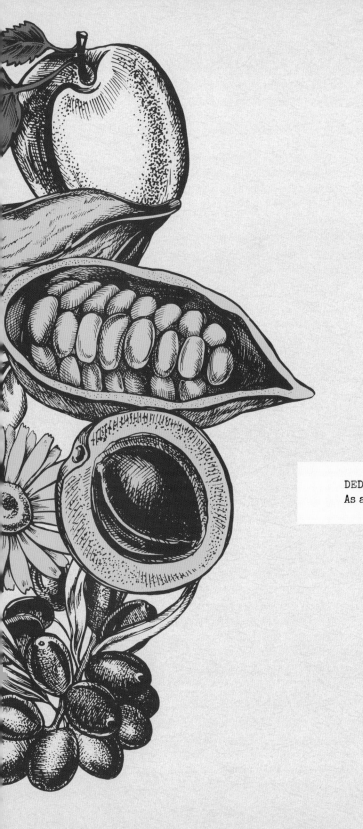

Contents

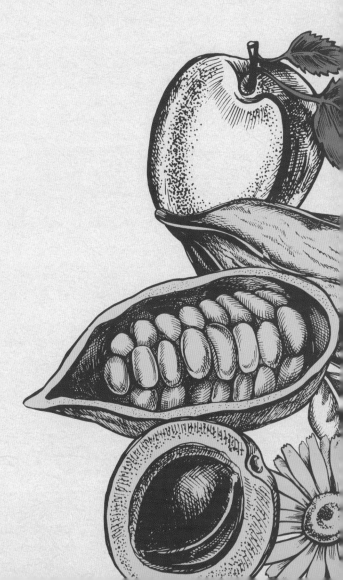

Introduction

I first became interested in making soap from scratch when my son was a toddler suffering from multiple allergies and eczema. It was difficult to find an allergen-free soap he could tolerate, so I set out to learn how to make one especially for him.

Upon researching the craft, however, I quickly became intimidated. Lye sounded too scary to handle! Reading about SAP numbers and lye calculators confused me. I just wanted to make a simple natural soap for my little boy; I wasn't looking for complicated.

Eventually, I discovered a book at my local library that walked me through the process in a way I could understand. Since I was still wary of handling lye at the time, I roped my husband into helping with the first batch of soap. We carefully measured, heated and mixed, then started stirring the soap by hand. After an hour or so, it didn't look much different, but we poured it into our unlined homemade wooden mold anyway. Needless to say, that wasn't a good idea! Our soap leaked right out of the mold and onto my basement floor.

The next several batches also failed to set up until I stumbled upon an early soapmaking website called Miller's Homemade Soapmaking Pages and learned about immersion blenders. We bought one to try out that very evening. To our delight, the same recipe that had failed us several times turned out perfectly! From that point on, I was officially bitten by the soapmaking bug.

My goal with this book is to make soapmaking approachable. By following the instructions within these pages carefully, you will be able to make a successful batch of soap and then glean the information needed to tailor the recipes to further suit your family's needs and likes.

I know how tough it is to deal with family members with allergies or how it feels to see a great looking recipe only to realize it contains a completely unobtainable ingredient, so a primary goal while writing this book was to make sure to include plenty of substitution options. Of course, I can't anticipate everyone's needs and budgets, so for that reason, I included Making Oil Substitutions on page 16 to help you learn to make substitutions on your own.

Natural is a huge buzzword these days and means different things to different people. In this book, the recipes are naturally scented with essential oils and rely solely on botanicals and clays to provide natural color. I'm especially excited to share the Photo Gallery of Natural Colorants on pages 146 to 154 that demonstrates natural doesn't have to be boring!

It was truly an enjoyable experience to write this book and I hope that you find it helpful in every way. If you run into any problems or questions with a recipe or wonder about a soapmaking topic I didn't address, feel free to write me through my website, TheNerdyFarmWife.com.

How to Use This Book

This book is divided into four key sections.

In Part 1, Getting Started Making Simple Natural Soaps, I give the basic information you need to begin your soapmaking journey or pick up some tips if you're not new to the craft. We'll start off by briefly talking about the benefits of making your own soap, then discuss lye—why we need it and things you should keep in mind when using it. You'll also learn important details to know about soapmaking in general, such as what kinds of equipment and molds you'll need, how to make substitutions in the recipes, the best way to clean up after making soap and how to cure and store your finished creations.

After that, I describe exactly how to make cold process soap, with step-by-step photos to help guide your first batches. Almost every recipe in this book (except for Vanilla Bean & Egg Yolk Soap, page 83) can be made using the hot process method instead of cold process, and in How to Convert Cold Process Recipes to Hot Process on page 22, I explain exactly how to adjust a recipe if you prefer making soap in a slow cooker.

From there, we dive into Part 2, the Recipes section, where I share 50 recipes, starting with the most basic bars then working through to soaps made with herbs, milk, honey and other completely natural ingredients. One unique thing you may notice about this book is that none of the recipes contain palm oil, a controversial ingredient whose production is linked to environmental and human rights issues. Instead, it's been replaced by vegetable butters, lard, tallow or blends of other oils. Most of the recipes require commonly found oils, but I've also included plenty of substitution options.

Part 3, Techniques and Tips to Take Your Soapmaking to the Next Level, is my favorite part and where things really get fun! I spent months testing dozens of botanicals and clays, recording how they performed in soap and comparing how they look when added to the lye solution, stirred into oils or added at trace. In this section, you'll find a photo gallery so you can get a visual on how a particular color might look in your soaps.

Other topics covered in this section include adding and blending essential oils, how to include nourishing herbal infusions and teas in your soap, plus several methods of enhancing your recipes with milk. Do you want to add layers or simple swirls in your soap for visual interest? You can find full directions with step-by-step photos in this section. You'll also discover how easy it is to dress up your soaps with stamps, impression mats, textured tops and botanical toppings.

Sometimes soap doesn't turn out as planned. It happens to all of us! In Part 4, Troubleshooting, you'll find some common problems that soapmakers occasionally run into, along with tips to help prevent those problems from happening to you. At the end of this section, you'll also find a list of resources to help you find the supplies you might not be able to source locally. My hope is that this book will be a useful starting guide for beginner soapmakers and a handy reference book for those who are more experienced.

Part 1

Getting Started Making
Simple Natural Soaps

Besides being a practical DIY skill to know, soapmaking is also a fun way to express yourself creatively. It's a hobby that produces a useful item that never fails to be welcomed by family and friends. Virtually everyone loves a good bar of handmade soap!

One of the most outstanding attributes of handcrafted soap is that it's kinder to your skin than most store-bought bars. When you make your own soap from scratch, glycerin, a natural byproduct of soapmaking, is distributed throughout each bar. Glycerin is highly beneficial and helps keep skin supple and moisturized. The companies that produce commercially made soap separate out the glycerin and sell it as a manufacturing commodity, which is one reason why those with sensitive skin may find store-bought soaps drying.

If you have allergies, fragrance sensitivities or certain ingredients you avoid for ethical or religious reasons, then making your own soap from scratch is the ideal way to make sure nothing harmful or unwanted gets on your skin.

When you're the one in charge of the entire soapmaking process from start to finish, you can know with full certainty that your family and friends are getting the purest and best product you can provide.

WHY WE NEED LYE AND HOW TO HANDLE IT SAFELY

A few generations ago, our great-great-grandmothers made their own lye, called potash, using wood ashes and water. They combined this highly caustic substance with fat rendered from butchered animals and boiled the mixture over an outdoor fire for many hours until a soft soap was formed. While this resulted in a truly natural soap, it was also difficult to control the quality of the final product.

These days, we have manufactured substitutes to replace that wood-ash solution. Sodium hydroxide, also called caustic soda or lye, is used to create solid bars of soap, while potassium hydroxide is used to make liquid soaps. With these standardized ingredients, the guesswork has been removed and modern soapmakers can reliably produce batch after batch of gentle, balanced soap.

Many crafty types find themselves interested in making their own soaps, but are concerned about handling lye. They often wonder if it's possible to make soap without it.

The short answer to this question is no. By definition, soap is what you end up with when fats and oils are combined with a highly caustic solution, no matter if it's our great-grandmother's potash or our modern-day sodium hydroxide.

When lye meets oils and fats, a chemical reaction occurs that changes both substances. Once that reaction is complete, you no longer have oils or lye; you've created soap! If made correctly, no lye is left in the final product. It's all used up and transformed on a molecular level during the process of converting the oils into soap.

By checking the label of your favorite store-bought soaps, you'll see that most are made using this method as well. You're likely to find words like sodium cocoate or sodium tallowate in the ingredient list. Those are just fancy ways of describing coconut oil or tallow (animal fat) that has reacted with sodium hydroxide (lye). Sometimes, labels may list ingredients such as saponified coconut oil or saponified olive oil. Saponified is another way to describe oils or fats that have been turned into soap after being exposed to lye.

If your favorite commercially produced soap doesn't list anything like that on the label, then it's likely made with one or more lather-producing synthetic detergents, such as sodium laureth sulfate or sodium lauryl sulfate, instead.

LYE SAFETY TIPS

If you decide to venture into soapmaking, follow standard safety precautions to help reduce the risk of serious harm. Like other household chemicals, lye can be dangerous if handled improperly, but you will rarely encounter issues if you work in a thoughtful and careful manner.

Lye should be used only by responsible adults. Never use it around children or pets.

Wear safety goggles, long sleeves and gloves during soapmaking sessions. Lye solution and fresh soap batter can cause serious damage to your eyes and painful burns on your skin. If this happens, rinse repeatedly with generous amounts of cold water for several minutes. Seek medical attention promptly for eye contact and large burns.

Sodium hydroxide is available in pellets, granules or flakes. All work equally well to make soap, though extra care is needed when working with flakes, as they tend to emit powder into the air that can be breathed in, irritating the lungs more easily. If dry lye spills on a surface in your work area, carefully brush off as much as you can, then wipe over the area with a damp cloth several times.

Always pour lye slowly into water that's room temperature or colder. By adding water to dry lye or pouring lye into hot water you risk overheating and producing a volcano effect. For this reason, it's a good idea to mix the lye solution in your kitchen sink. If any accidents occur, they will be contained and much easier to clean up than a countertop spill.

Avoid breathing in fumes. When lye is first mixed with water, it will form strong fumes. Work in a well-ventilated area such as outdoors, in front of a window or under an exhaust fan. Turn your head away as you stir. If you find yourself sensitive to the fumes, consider wearing a respirator.

Clearly label containers intended for mixing and holding lye solution with a skull and crossbones symbol, and when filled, place in a safe location out of reach of children and pets. By doing this, even non-readers will realize the contents should not be handled or ingested. Just like bleach and other strong household chemicals, lye can be fatal if accidentally swallowed.

Use the proper equipment. Never use aluminum when making soap, as it will combine with lye to form a toxic reaction. Mix your lye solution in a heavy-duty heatproof plastic container (look for recycle symbol number 5 on the bottom) or stainless steel, as glass has the potential to shatter. Stir the lye solution with a heavy-duty silicone or heatproof plastic spatula or spoon. Have separate equipment for measuring and mixing lye and do not reuse them for food preparation.

Remember that these are worst-case scenarios. Soap is made every day by people all over the world without incident. Caution when handling is wise and necessary, but don't allow fear to keep you from trying out a rewarding new pastime.

LYE CALCULATORS

An important tool for soapmakers, lye calculators are used to determine the exact amount of lye needed to create a balanced bar of soap.

Oils and fats are unique in their individual makeup and require differing amounts of lye (sodium hydroxide) to turn into soap. For example, olive oil requires roughly twice as much lye to saponify (turn into soap) than jojoba oil. If you decided to replace the olive oil in a recipe with jojoba instead and didn't change the lye amount, you may end up with too much lye.

There are several lye calculators available to use for free online and while they vary somewhat in their layout and appearance, they all return reliable results, as far as how much lye you need for the amount of oils in a recipe. You can find a listing of online lye calculators in the resource section in the back of this book.

My preference is to use the one found at www.TheSage.com for its straightforward simplicity, so that's the one I refer to in the instructions below.

HOW TO CHECK A SOAP RECIPE WITH A LYE CALCULATOR

All new-to-you soap recipes, even ones in this book, should be double-checked with a lye calculator before making. Typing and printing errors happen, so taking a quick minute to make sure the recipe is correct will be time well spent.

STEP 1

Go to www.TheSage.com (my preferred online lye calculator) and click on the link that says Lye Calculator. You'll be presented with a form to fill in.

STEP 2

Select whether you want to work in ounces or grams, double check that the lye type is sodium Hydroxide (NaOH), which is the type of lye needed to make solid bars of soap, then scroll down to the big list of oils.

STEP 3

Input the oils listed in the recipe that you're interested in making. As an example, if the recipe requires 15 ounces (425 g) of olive oil and 5 ounces (142 g) of coconut oil, and you're working in ounces, then input the number 15 inside the box beside olive oil and the number 5 inside the box beside coconut oil. Scroll to the bottom and click the Calculate Lye button.

STEP 4

A new screen will appear with the results, which break down in the following way.

In the Liquids box, the calculator gives a range of liquid to use in your recipe. For our example recipe from step 3, it tells us we need approximately 5 to 8 ounces (142 to 227 g) of liquid. If you use the lower number, your soap will reach trace and set up in the mold more quickly than usual. Sometimes, this is a good thing, such as when making castile soap; other times, the soap batter will move too rapidly to easily work with. The lower range is not recommended for beginners. The higher end of the water range, in this case 8 ounces (227 g), will give you plenty of time for swirls or more intricate details, but will also take longer to reach trace and firm up in soap molds, plus may need a slightly longer cure time to permit excess water to evaporate. The middle of the range, in this case 6.5 ounces (185 g), is a happy medium that should give good results. An even easier way to determine water amount for your recipe is by employing a handy tip learned from Amanda Aaron of the Lovin Soap website (see Resources page 187) and just use twice as much water as lye.

Beside the Liquids box, you'll see a Fats & Oils section that breaks down your recipe's oils into percentages. This is helpful to compare against the recommendations in the Soapmaking Oils and Fats and Their Properties on page 14. While those guidelines are suggestions only and shouldn't be taken as gospel, if you see a recipe requiring 85 percent jojoba oil, you'll know there might be an error somewhere.

Right beside Fats & Oils is a lye table. In most cases, you want the lye amount to fall in the 5 to 8 percent range.

Once you've verified that the recipe you're interested in has a safe amount of lye, you're ready to make your soap.

SOAPMAKING EQUIPMENT

You'll need the following equipment to make soap. While experts aren't in total agreement on the matter, I personally do not recommend using the same tools and containers for both soapmaking and cooking, especially containers used to measure and mix lye and essential oils.

Rubber or latex gloves, goggles and a **long-sleeved shirt** will keep hands, eyes and arms protected. Do not handle lye, lye solution or raw batter without putting on this important safety gear first. Never get too complacent about safety when it comes to soapmaking, no matter your level of experience and expertise.

Dry lye can be weighed using **a small plastic, glass or stainless steel container.** You could also use small disposable bathroom cups for this purpose.

The liquid for the lye solution can be weighed in **a stainless steel or heavy-duty plastic container** with a recycle number 5 symbol on the bottom. Because the lye solution can heat to over 200°F (93°C), glass is not recommended, as the quick temperature change can cause it to shatter.

Oils and the lye solution can be mixed together in **a medium-sized container or mixing bowl.** My local DIY store has heavy-duty 2.5-quart (2.37-L) plastic paint mixing buckets that work perfectly for this purpose. You can also use Pyrex at this point since it won't be directly exposed to the temperature fluctuation of the lye solution. Stainless steel, enamel-lined pots or the ceramic liner that comes with a slow cooker are other options. Don't use aluminum, cast iron or non-stick containers or utensils when making soap as they can react adversely to the lye.

Ingredients should be weighed with **an accurate digital scale.** I use two different scales, a standard kitchen scale for weighing water, oils and lye and a more precise scale for measuring small amounts of extra additives and essential oils. For years I only owned a digital kitchen scale and it worked just fine. Check your local store that carries kitchen supplies for a reasonably priced scale.

A thermometer is needed for checking oil and lye solution temperatures. A standard candy thermometer, designated for soapmaking only, works well for this purpose. When you're ready to upgrade, a handheld infrared thermometer is much easier to use and well worth the investment. Check your local hardware or DIY store for a reasonably priced infrared thermometer.

An immersion blender, also called a stick blender, speeds up the length of stirring time from hours to mere minutes. Cheaper isn't always better with this purchase since inexpensive motors tend to overheat and need replacing more often.

You'll also need **a soap mold** to pour the soap batter in. This can be a standard style loaf mold or individual molds. See the following section for more in-depth information on molds.

SOAP MOLDS

Each recipe in this book, except the shaving soap on page 123, will yield roughly 2.5 pounds (1.13 kg) of soap.

Most of the soaps were developed and tested using a commonly found regular silicone loaf mold that measures 3.5" × 8" × 2.5" (8.9 × 20.3 × 6.4 cm) and holds up to 44 ounces (1.25 kg) or a homemade wooden mold built with similar dimensions.

Round soaps were made in a silicone two-piece column mold with cavity dimensions of $9^3/4$" (25 cm) length × $2^3/4$" (7 cm) diameter, while specially shaped soaps were made in a variety of individual silicone molds.

If you're anxious to make your first batch of soap, but haven't gotten around to purchasing a mold yet, an empty clean milk carton makes a great starter mold. Simply cut off the carton's top, make a batch of soap and pour it directly into your newly created mold. Allow it to stay in the mold for 24 hours before peeling away the paper.

SOAPMAKING OILS & FATS & THEIR PROPERTIES

Vegetable oils and butters, along with animal fats, can all be used for making soap. Over the next few pages, I share some of the more commonly available kinds, plus some suggested usage rates to consider when making substitutions or creating your own recipes. Treat these numbers as general guidelines only and don't be afraid to experiment outside of the lines.

ALMOND OIL, SWEET (*PRUNUS AMYGDALUS DULCIS*)—high in vitamin E and helps to nourish and moisturize dry skin. Use up to 15 to 20 percent in a soap recipe.

APRICOT KERNEL OIL (*PRUNUS ARMENIACA*)—a nutritious oil, rich in essential fatty acids. It has similar properties as sweet almond oil in a soap recipe, making it a great substitute for those allergic to almonds. Apricot kernel oil is especially good for dry or mature skin. Use up to 15 to 20 percent in a soap recipe.

ARGAN OIL (*ARGANIA SPINOSA*)—a luxurious oil pressed from argan nuts, rich in antioxidants and valued for its anti-inflammatory and anti-aging properties in skin care. It's also a popular addition to shampoo bar recipes for its ability to promote healthy hair growth. Use up to or around 10 percent in a soap recipe.

AVOCADO OIL (*PERSEA GRATISSIMA*)—a rich oil, full of essential fatty acids and carotenoids. Since it's pressed from the fruit, it's a great choice for those with tree nut allergies. While the unrefined version of avocado oil contains more moisturizing compounds, keep in mind that its dark green color may affect how natural colorants look in your soap, enhancing greens, but potentially muddying other shades. Use up to 15 to 20 percent in a soap recipe.

BABASSU OIL (*ORBIGNYA OLEIFERA*)—a moisturizing and anti-inflammatory solid oil high in lauric acid. It behaves similarly to coconut oil in soap, making it a perfect substitute for those who are allergic to coconuts. While the oil is derived from the babassu palm tree that grows in South America, it should not be confused as a product of the modern palm oil industry that's currently surrounded by many environmental and humanitarian issues. Babassu oil can be used up to or around 30 percent in a soap recipe, though just like coconut oil, it can be drying if used in high amounts.

CASTOR OIL (*RICINUS COMMUNIS*)—a thick oil high in ricinoleic acid. A small amount, or around 5 to 7 percent, of castor oil can be added to any soap recipe to help boost bubbles. Many shampoo bars contain even higher amounts (around 15 percent) to ensure a satisfactory lathering experience. Some soapmakers report that higher amounts of castor oil causes their soap to feel sticky or tacky, though I've not personally experienced that in amounts up to 15 percent.

COCOA BUTTER (*THEOBROMA CACAO*)—a solid fat produced from cocoa beans that adds hardness and a creamy lather to soaps. Unrefined cocoa butter is more nutritive than the refined version, but contributes a light chocolate scent to finished soaps. This attribute works well for soaps such as Milk Chocolate Mint (page 84) and Coffee Bean Scrub Bar (page 140), but for other soaps such as Grandma's Yellow Roses (page 47), you may want to use the unscented refined version to avoid masking delicate floral scents. Use up to or around 15 percent in a soap recipe, as too much cocoa butter can cause your soap to crack.

COCONUT OIL (*COCOS NUCIFERA*)—high in lauric acid, coconut oil is essential to most soap recipes for its notable lathering properties. (If allergic to coconut, babassu oil will provide similar properties, albeit at a higher price point.) While virgin coconut oil can be used in soap recipes, its lovely scent will not survive the soapmaking process. Because of its cleansing properties when added to soap, those with sensitive or dry skin may find it irritating in high amounts unless the recipe includes a higher superfat (see page 18 on more about superfat). Use up to or around 30 percent in a soap recipe, less for more sensitive skin. You can also use coconut oil at 100 percent when coupled with a higher superfat. See page 34 for Pure Coconut Oil Bars and page 93 for Cambrian Blue Cooling Salt Bars.

HEMPSEED OIL (*CANNABIS INDICA*)—a nutritious seed oil high in essential fatty acids that heals and soothes damaged skin. Unrefined hemp oil's deep green tint carries over beautifully into finished soap, enhancing the color of any natural green colorants used in the recipe. Use up to or around 15 percent in a soap recipe.

JOJOBA OIL (*SIMMONDSIA CHINENSIS*)—a liquid plant wax that helps soften and smooth dry skin, while regulating oily and acne-prone skin. It adds shine and conditions hair, making it a great addition to shampoo bar recipes. Use up to or around 10 percent in a soap recipe.

KOKUM BUTTER (*GARCINIA INDICA*)—a naturally white hard butter that can usually be equally substituted for cocoa butter in a recipe. It's a natural source of stearic acid, making it a great addition to help harden palm-free recipes. Aim to use up to 15 percent in a recipe. Shave soap recipes sometimes use even higher amounts of kokum butter to provide the large amounts of stearic acid needed to create a dense lather for shaving.

KUKUI NUT OIL (*ALEURITES MOLUCCANA*)—a nourishing and anti-inflammatory oil used to relieve the symptoms of skin problems such as eczema and psoriasis. Use around 5 to 10 percent in a soap recipe to add a luxurious and creamy feel.

LARD—a solid fat rendered from pigs. It makes an excellent substitute for palm oil in palm-free recipes, adds some hardness to soap, a creamy lather and skin conditioning properties. If you avoid pork products, you can use beef tallow in place of lard in most instances, or in some cases, kokum or cocoa butter instead. While you can use up to 100 percent lard to make soap, it does best when used up to 30 or 40 percent in a recipe and combined with other oils such as olive, coconut and castor.

MANGO BUTTER (*MANGIFERA INDICA*)—a solid fat that nourishes, moisturizes and repairs dry or damaged skin. It adds a creamy feel but not a lot of hardness when used in soap. Use from 5 to 15 percent in a soap recipe.

OLIVE OIL (*OLEA EUROPAEA*)—a skin-friendly oil widely used as a base ingredient in most soap recipes. Soaps high in olive oil start off soft, but cure to hardness over time. On its own, olive oil produces few bubbles so is often combined with coconut and sometimes castor oil for more satisfactory lather. While it's generally well tolerated by most people, if you're allergic to olive oil, rice bran oil makes for a fairly good substitute in most recipes. There are several types of olive oil available including extra virgin, pure, refined and pomace. All of these work equally well in soap recipes, though pomace is prone to increasing trace. Also, keep in mind that the dark green color of extra virgin olive oil can muddy natural colorants, so you may want to use a lighter colored variety in recipes where color is important. You can use olive oil in any amount in a recipe, all the way up to 100 percent.

PALM OIL (*ELAEIS GUINEENSIS*)—a commonly used soapmaking oil that adds hardness to soap recipes. Because its production is surrounded by environmental and human rights controversy, it's not used in this book, but instead replaced with vegetable butters, animal fats or other oil combinations. Palm oil is often used at rates of around 20 to 30 percent in a recipe.

RICE BRAN OIL (*ORYZA SATIVA*)—a nutritious oil and rich source of the antioxidant squalene. It can be used as a substitute for all or part of the olive oil in a recipe. It's normally used up to or around 15 to 20 percent in a soap recipe, but can be used up to 100 percent if needed.

ROSEHIP SEED OIL (*ROSA RUBIGINOSA*)—a regenerative oil, naturally high in vitamins, carotenoids and other beneficial compounds. Because of its relatively high cost, it's used in small amounts in soap recipes intended for weathered, aged or problematic skin. Use up to or around 5 to 10 percent in a soap recipe.

SHEA BUTTER (*VITELLARIA PARADOXA* OR *BUTYROSPERMUM PARKII*)—a solid fat made from the nuts of the shea (karite) tree. High in unsaponifiable nutrients (beneficial elements that remain in the finished soap), shea butter also contributes a small amount of hardness to palm-free recipes. Use up to or around 15 percent in a soap recipe.

SUNFLOWER OIL (*HELIANTHUS ANNUUS*)—a light, skin-friendly oil high in lecithin and vitamins A, D and E. Look specifically for high-oleic oil for the longest shelf life, but any recipe that contains sunflower oil will benefit from the addition of rosemary antioxidants (rosemary extract). (See Shelf Life of Soap & Extending It on page 17.) Use up to 15 to 20 percent in a soap recipe. Too much sunflower oil in a recipe will make an overly soft soap.

TALLOW—a solid fat usually rendered from beef, though you can find other types of tallow such as deer or goat. It makes an excellent substitute for palm oil in palm-free recipes, adds hardness to your finished soap, a good lather and skin conditioning properties. If you avoid animal products, you may be able to substitute some of the tallow in a recipe with kokum or cocoa butter. While you can use up to 100 percent tallow in a recipe, it does best when used up to 30 or 40 percent in a recipe and combined with other oils such as olive, coconut and castor.

TAMANU OIL (*CALOPHYLLUM INOPHYLLUM*)—a thick dark green nut oil traditionally used to treat a variety of skin ailments. A small amount (around 5 percent of a recipe) makes a nice addition to soaps intended for those with eczema, psoriasis and other such conditions.

MAKING OIL SUBSTITUTIONS

While at least one substitution option is provided for most of the recipes in this book, here are some further guidelines to help when changing up the oils in a recipe.

If you're allergic to coconut oil, babassu makes a good substitute. It requires slightly less lye to saponify (turn into soap) than coconut oil. Always run recipe changes through a lye calculator (see page 11), but it may be handy to know that for the recipes in this book, substituting babassu for coconut will almost always result in the recipe's required lye amount being lowered slightly by 0.5 ounces (14 g). The only caveat to using babassu instead of coconut relates to salt bars, as ones made with babassu don't lather nearly as well as the coconut version.

In most cases, olive oil can be equally substituted with rice bran oil without a need to change the amount of lye in the recipe, though the resulting soap may turn out slightly different than described.

Castor oil is fantastic for encouraging bubbly lather in soap, and ideally I'd include it in almost every recipe. Since it can be hard to source in some areas, it can be omitted. You can usually substitute another oil, such as sweet almond, sunflower, hemp, avocado or even more olive oil. None of these will help with lather like castor though, so the final soap's properties will be somewhat affected. Run any oil changes through a lye calculator (see page 11) since the lye amount is likely to change.

Shea and mango butter can be interchanged readily in any of the recipes in this book. If those butters aren't available or allergies are an issue, try using cocoa or kokum butter, or tallow or lard in their place. Double check with a lye calculator (page 11), but in most cases the lye will remain unchanged or only slightly increase by 0.5 ounces (14 g).

SHELF LIFE OF SOAP & EXTENDING IT

Soap doesn't mold or spoil in the usual sense of the word. Instead, the oils contained within start to oxidize and age and eventually become rancid. There's no exact way to predict how long a bar of soap will stay fresh, though a common recommendation is to use handmade soap within one year. You'll know a soap is past its prime if it starts smelling like old vegetable oil.

Another indicator of old soap is the appearance of DOS, which stands for dreaded orange spots. These spots are usually shades of orange, brown or yellow and often have an unpleasant smell. They indicate that significant rancidity is going on with the soap. While the soap is still technically safe to use, it's not always pleasant to do so.

The following tips will help you better avoid DOS from happening prematurely to your soaps. Use the freshest, best quality oils that you can. Old oils will make a soap that ages faster. Distilled water is preferable to tap water, as the latter can sometimes contain minerals or impurities that affects soap in adverse ways. Store your soap loaves and bars in a non-humid area, away from direct sunlight and heat. Soap needs to stay cool and dry, with good air circulation.

Kevin Dunn, scientist and author of *Scientific Soapmaking: The Chemistry of the Cold Process*, recommends using 0.1 percent of the oil weight in rosemary antioxidants (also called rosemary oleoresin extract, or ROE) to help extend shelf life in natural soaps. For the recipes in this book, that translates to slightly less than 1 gram. Following that recommendation, I add rosemary antioxidants to almost every batch of soap I make, being especially vigilant during periods of high humidity.

To add rosemary antioxidants to your soap recipes, measure out 1 gram (which is roughly 40 drops or ¼ teaspoon) and stir it into your warmed oils, before adding the lye solution. It will not change the color or scent of your finished soap.

As you can see, the shelf life of soap is highly dependent on the ingredients used, how the soap is stored and whether you add rosemary antioxidants to your soap or not. Don't automatically feel that your soap is expired once it reaches one year of age as it may last for several years longer.

HOW TO READ RECIPES

The recipes in this book are broken down into the following sections.

RECIPE TITLE AND SOME FEATURE CHARACTERISTICS—here, I'll tell a little bit about the ingredients in the recipe, highlighting any interesting or important information you may need to know.

INGREDIENTS—All soap recipes require lye (sodium hydroxide for solid bars, potassium hydroxide for liquid soaps), some type of liquid to activate the lye, plus oils and fats for the lye solution to react with. Different types of oils require different amounts of lye to fully turn into soap, so you can't just substitute any oil or butter for another without potentially altering the amount of lye needed. I've given several substitution options in each recipe, but you'll still want to use a lye calculator to double check the recipe, especially if you make any changes. (See page 11 for more on lye calculators and page 16 for more on making oil substitutions.)

Most measurements are given by weight (ounces and grams), even the liquid portions, to ensure accuracy. Percentages are given for those who need to resize the recipes to fit in differently sized molds. Even slight variations in oils and lye can have a big impact in soap, so be sure to use an accurate digital scale to weigh out those critical ingredients.

Some types of scales may have difficulty calculating very small weight amounts, such as needed for measuring out essential oils in a recipe. Because essential oils vary in density depending on molecular makeup, growing conditions and supplier, they also differ widely in viscosity and weight. For example, 1 teaspoon (5 ml) of peru balsam essential oil weighs roughly 4 grams, while 1 teaspoon (5 ml) of vetiver essential oil weighs roughly 2.9 grams. I've given a rough volume equivalent in recipes that use especially tiny amounts of an essential oil if you need it, but ideally, you should measure by weight whenever possible, using a small pocket scale that measures to 0.01 gram accuracy.

Extra additives, such as oatmeal, honey and natural colorants require less precision and do not need to be weighed. They are listed by teaspoon, tablespoon or other units of volume measurement.

Many of the recipes in this book have a reduced water amount to ensure that the resulting soaps release more easily from their molds. (Without the hardening properties of palm oil, palm-free soaps tend to start off softer, but will further harden over cure time.) If you find that your soap batter thickens and reaches trace too quickly, add an additional 0.5 ounce (14 g) of distilled water to the recipe.

ALL ABOUT SUPERFATTING

In the presence of heat and water, soap is created when molecules of lye match up with molecules of fats and oils. They then chemically react to become a new substance—soap, plus glycerin. If you calculated a soap recipe so that you had precisely enough lye for the amount of oils and fats available, it would be considered a zero superfat because no extra fats (or oils) would be left unchanged by the lye. While this is acceptable, especially for laundry soaps, it leaves no wiggle room for human error in measurement or slight natural variations between oil values. A zero percent superfatted soap isn't very moisturizing either. For this reason, an extra amount of oil or fat is calculated into soap recipes, which is called superfatting. With a few noted exceptions, the soaps in this book tend to fall between a 5 and 7 percent superfat. This is generally considered a good balanced range to create gentle and moisturizing soaps. While some level of superfat is desirable, it's possible to have too much of a good thing. Soaps that have an excess of extra oil, or superfat, will be overly soft and gooey when wet.

EXTRAS—These are the small amounts of additives (see page 161), natural colorants (see page 145) and essential oils (see pages 158) scattered throughout the ingredient list that help give the soap its unique characteristics. For instance, a lavender oatmeal soap recipe contains lavender essential oil and ground oatmeal. It's okay to leave out or substitute any of the extras if you don't like that ingredient or don't have it on hand, keeping in mind that it will change the final soap's characteristics. For example, if you decide you want to make peppermint oatmeal soap instead of lavender, just leave out the lavender essential oil and put peppermint essential oil in its place.

Or you might decide to replace the oatmeal with poppy seeds to create lavender poppy seed soap. You could also leave out the essential oils and oatmeal altogether and make a plain basic bar. Extras are added in such small amounts, they don't affect the overall ratio of lye and oils, so feel free to get creative with them without worrying that you need to adjust the amount of lye used.

DIRECTIONS—After the ingredient list, you'll find abbreviated instructions on how to make the recipe. Be sure that you're completely familiar with the entire soapmaking process as shown on the pages to follow, since the recipes only include an overview. Directions given are for the cold process version of the recipe, but instructions can be found on page 22 if you'd like to convert any of the recipes to hot process.

SUBSTITUTIONS & TIPS—At the end of each recipe, you'll find at least one substitution to better accommodate those with allergies or ingredient limitations or a tip that will be helpful to know when making the recipe.

COLD PROCESS SOAPMAKING DIRECTIONS

Before you make your first batch of soap, read through the following steps carefully. Remember that measurements are by weight, including the water or liquid portion. You must use an accurate scale to make soap. Always wear gloves and goggles no matter how many years you've been making soap or how comfortable you feel with the process.

STEP 1

Select the recipe that you want to make. Whether it's one from this book or one you found elsewhere, it's a good idea to double check with a lye calculator (see page 11) to make sure the lye amount is correct. Typing and printing errors happen, so taking a quick minute to make sure the recipe is correct will be time well spent.

Assemble all of the ingredients for the soap, along with all safety gear and equipment needed. (See page 12 for a list of required equipment.) Double-check your bottle of lye by gently shaking it. If you hear clumps rattling around, that indicates that moisture has found its way inside and the lye may not measure accurately. Prepare the mold, lining if needed (see page 13 for more on choosing and lining soap molds).

Weigh out the water or liquid portion of the recipe into a heatproof heavy duty plastic or stainless steel container, and set it down into your kitchen sink or other spot near a source of fresh air or an exhaust fan.

Put on your gloves and goggles, then weigh out the amount of lye needed for the recipe. Slowly pour the lye into the water or other liquid and gently stir with a silicone or heavy duty plastic spoon or spatula. The mixture will quickly reach over 200°F (93°C), so handle carefully. Stir until dissolved, making sure no residual layer of lye granules remains at the bottom of the container. Work in a well-ventilated area and avoid directly breathing in the temporary, but strong, lye fumes. Set the lye solution aside in a safe place out of reach of children and pets, and let it cool for about 30 to 40 minutes or until the temperature drops to around 100 to 110°F (38 to 43°C).

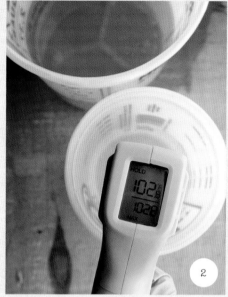

STEP 2

While the lye solution cools, weigh out the oils, butters and solid fats needed for the recipe. Any essential oils, colorants and additional additives required for the recipe should also be measured at this time and then set aside until needed. Melt solid fats such as coconut oil, butters, tallow and lard in a double boiler before adding to the other oils in your mixing container. Heat the oils until warmer, if necessary, until they're around 100 to 110°F (38 to 43°C). The temperatures of the lye solution and oils don't have to be exactly within that range. Some soapmakers prefer to work cooler than the numbers I give, allowing lye and oils to settle to room temperature before mixing. Others prefer to work at warmer temperatures, up to 125°F (52°C). When working with milk, honey or other ingredients containing natural sugars, such as food purees and juices, you will often work with cooler temperatures to help prevent overheating. Occasionally, you will need to work with much hotter temperatures, as in the case of beeswax. (See Honey & Beeswax Soap on page 109.) With time and practice, you'll develop your own temperature preferences.

STEP 3

Pour the lye solution into the oils. When you first place the immersion blender into the unmixed oil and lye solution mixture, tilt it slightly sideways to allow any trapped bubbles to escape. Straighten it again and make sure it's fully submerged before turning on. Hand stir with the immersion blender (powered off) for around 20 to 30 seconds, then turn the immersion blender on and mix the soap batter, alternating every 30 seconds with hand stirring to prevent excessive air bubbles and the blender's motor from burning out. Continue mixing until a light trace is reached. This could take anywhere from 2 to 10 minutes, depending on the recipe. Trace means that the soap batter is thick enough to leave a faint, fleeting imprint when it's drizzled across itself.

WHAT DOES TRACE MEAN?

When a soap mixture has reached trace, that means it has fully emulsified and thickened just enough to hold an outline, or tracing, for a few seconds when you drizzle some of the soap batter across the surface of itself. The photo for step 3 shows soap at a medium trace, which is what I usually like to work with. A thin trace is fully emulsified, but won't show a visible imprint like medium trace does, so it can be tricky for beginner soapmakers to easily recognize. Thin trace is helpful if you want to make fancy swirls and designs within your soap. A thick trace is pudding-like and tends to be scooped or plopped into the mold rather than poured. Soap with a thick trace is best for making textured tops (see page 168). It also tends to set up quicker, making the finished soap ready to unmold slightly sooner.

STEP 4

Once trace is reached, hand stir in any extra ingredients such as essential oils, natural colorants, honey, oatmeal and such, then pour the soap batter into the prepared mold. If desired, texturize the top or gently press dried flowers or other botanicals (see page 168) for decoration. The soap will still be caustic at this point, so keep your gloves and goggles on while handling it. Cover the mold with a sheet of wax or freezer paper and then the mold top if it has one. Insulate the mold with a towel or quilt to retain heat. If your soap contains milk, honey or other items with natural sugars, it will tend to heat up more than other soaps so you may want to leave it uncovered. You could also put the filled mold in the refrigerator to avoid gel phase altogether. An alternative idea is to use smaller individual molds, which release heat faster than loaf molds.

WHAT IS GEL PHASE?

Once soap is mixed and poured into the mold, it will begin to heat itself to a higher temperature due to the chemical reaction still going on between the oils and lye. As this happens, the appearance of the soap changes. Usually starting in the center of the mold, the soap turns darker and develops a jelly-like (or gel-like) appearance. This often alarms new soapmakers who think they've done something wrong. Rest assured that gel phase is a perfectly normal part of the soapmaking process and a good thing! One of the benefits of letting your soap naturally go through gel phase is that it helps many natural colorants show up more brightly and results in a soap that hardens up faster and releases from the mold more easily.

In some cases, however, gel phase isn't desired. Soaps made with milk, honey and other ingredients containing natural sugars will turn varying shades of brown when they go through gel phase. Some soapmakers prefer this look, while others strive for a lighter, whiter soap. To prevent gel phase, use cooler temperatures when making the soap and place the filled mold directly into a refrigerator or freezer for 24 hours. Remove the mold, and then allow it to sit undisturbed an additional two to three days, or until firm enough to unmold.

Sometimes, soap will heat up in the middle of the mold, but not along the edges. When this happens, a partial gel occurs, which is evident when the center of a cut bar is noticeably darker than the outside edges. You can read more about partial gel and how to prevent it on page 183 in the troubleshooting section of this book.

Allow the soap to stay in the mold for 24 to 48 hours or until the soap releases easily. It's okay to peek at your soap in the hours after pouring to make sure it's doing okay. If you see a crack developing, it means the soap is getting too hot and should be uncovered and possibly moved to a cooler area. Once you release the soap from the mold, slice it into bars, cure the bars for 3 to 4 weeks, and then you can choose to store, use or give them away!

HOW TO CONVERT A COLD PROCESS RECIPE INTO A HOT PROCESS RECIPE

The hot process (HP) method is similar to cold process (CP), with the addition of one extra step. Instead of mixing the soap batter to trace, adding extras (such as essential oils, honey, oatmeal, etc.), then pouring into a mold, the soap batter is mixed to trace, cooked in a slow cooker for around an hour, then the extras are added before spooning into a mold.

A primary benefit of hot process is that by cooking the soap you speed up the entire soapmaking process so your soap is ready to use sooner. While hot process soap is technically suitable to use once it cools, it still benefits from 2 to 3 weeks of cure time so excess water can evaporate out, leading to a longer lasting bar of soap.

Any cold process soap recipe in this book (except for Vanilla Bean & Egg Yolk Soap, page 83) can be made using the hot process method instead, with one important caveat in mind. The recipes in this book use a water discount, which means the normal water amount has been reduced somewhat to allow the soap to reach trace faster and firm up in a soap mold faster. This leads to a more satisfying soapmaking experience for most, plus reduces the chance of soda ash and glycerin rivers (see pages 184 and 183) from forming in cold process soap.

Use the following steps to convert any recipe in this book to hot process.

STEP 1

Increase the amount of water or liquid needed in the recipe to 10 ounces (283 g) to make sure that the soap doesn't dry out and get hard to work with while cooking. This rule applies to the 2.5 pound (1.13 kg) recipes designed specifically for this book and won't necessarily apply to recipes found elsewhere.

STEP 2

Mix the soap as per cold process instructions (pages 19 to 22), mixing until light trace. Because of the extra water, this step may take several minutes longer than usual. Once trace is reached, pour the soap batter into a slow cooker and turn the heat on low. Some slow cookers' older models may need to be preheated about 15 minutes first, if they're slow to warm up.

STEP 3

Cover the slow cooker and cook the soap on low for approximately one hour, checking every 15 minutes and stirring down if needed. The soap will go through several stages during this time. First, it will begin to separate, with visible puddles of liquid in some places (photo 3A), then it will start to expand in the slow cooker (photo 3B). Finally, it will turn gel-like and resemble petroleum jelly or glossy mashed potatoes when stirred (photos 3C and 4). At this point, the soap can be removed from the heat.

STEP 4

After the soap cools slightly, for around ten minutes or so, stir in any extras such as essential oils, honey, oatmeal or natural colorants. Be careful with honey as it can easily scorch upon contact with hot cooked soap. For best results, dilute the honey with an equal amount of warm water and carefully stir the mixture in once the soap has cooled for several minutes. To help the soap loosen up and become easier to work with, try stirring in 1 tablespoon (15 ml) of plain yogurt mixed with 1 tablespoon (15 ml) of hot water.

STEP 5

Spoon the soap into a mold and leave uncovered. Allow the soap to cool overnight, then remove from the mold and slice into bars. While you can use the soap right away, it will last longer if allowed to cure in the open air for 2 to 3 weeks before use.

TIPS FOR SAFELY CLEANING UP

For the first 24 hours or so, fresh soap batter is still caustic and contains unsaponified oils, which means care must be taken while cleaning up. While it seems easiest to just throw everything in the dishwasher upon completion, I learned from personal experience that very fresh soap batter acts similarly to thick grease in kitchen pipes and will eventually build up, causing plumbing issues.

One drain-safe way to approach the cleanup task is to set all of the mixing equipment and containers aside for 24 hours, safely out of reach of pets and children. Within that time, the oils will complete the saponification process and the remaining thin layer of soap can be easily washed away with warm water, after soaking for a short bit first if needed.

For an alternative method that requires no waiting, wipe out the inside of any equipment or containers that held soap batter with rags or paper towels as much as possible. Place the rags in a plastic grocery bag for final disposal in your trash can, making sure pets and children can't get into them. Since the soap is still caustic for around 24 hours after making, be sure to wear gloves and goggles the entire time. Containers that held lye and lye solution can be washed separately with plenty of clean running water while wearing gloves and goggles. Be sure these two containers are clearly marked, and don't use them for any purpose other than soapmaking.

CUTTING, CURING & STORING SOAPS

After the first 48 hours, your soap should be fully saponified, which means all of the lye has reacted with the oil and the soap should no longer be caustic. Gloves are not necessary to handle the soap after this point. Once the soap is hard enough to easily unmold, turn it out onto a sheet of wax or freezer paper. Sometimes the soap may still be on the soft side and easily dented when you gently press a fingertip on it. If that's the case, let it sit in the open air for another day or two before slicing a test piece from the end of the loaf. If it cuts easily, but isn't squishy, then you can go ahead and cut into bars. A common thickness for cutting soap bars is 1" (2.5 cm), while others prefer 1¼" (3 cm). Use a non-serrated kitchen knife for cutting soap. Another option is a vegetable crinkle cutter, commonly found in kitchen supply stores. The drawback to both options is that you must estimate where to cut the soap and it's difficult to get straight lines and consistent sizes. While they cost more, specially designed steel wire soap cutters are available that ensure perfectly uniform bars of soap (see the resources section).

Although saponification is complete and the soap is technically safe to use and try out after cutting into bars, it's best to let them go through a cure period of at least 3 to 4 weeks for cold process soap, or 2 to 3 weeks for hot process. Over this time, extra water content evaporates out, making it so the bars are denser and longer lasting when used. Soap naturally loses weight over cure time, indicating that the bars are curing as they should.

Soap should be stored out of direct sunlight and high heat. Humidity is the enemy of handmade soap, leading to a shorter shelf life (see page 17). Cure soap on sheets of wax paper or coated wire racks, turning occasionally so the bars cure evenly. After cure time, store in an area that gets good air circulation. I keep still-curing soaps on shelves in my home office, with older bars stored in an old hutch, turned into a makeshift soap storage cabinet.

Part 2

Recipes
The Simplest Basics

Plain and simple, these no-frills recipes are perfect for beginners or those seeking a basic palm-free soap recipe.

High in skin-nourishing olive oil, castile and bastille soaps are among the gentlest types of soap you can make. While they tend to lack significant lather and take an extra measure of patience because of the longer required cure time, they're ideal for mildly cleansing the most sensitive skin types.

Olive isn't the only oil that can be used at such high amounts in a recipe. Old-Fashioned Lye Soap (page 37) is made completely from tallow or lard, while Pure Coconut Oil Bars (page 34) offer an alternative vegan variation.

While single oil soaps are straightforward to make, most people prefer a recipe with a more balanced oil profile to ensure that the gentle cleansing comes along with a satisfying amount of lather plus long lasting hardness. If that sounds like your kind of soap, check out the customizable Basic Palm-Free Soap recipes found on pages 38 and 39.

Keep in mind that while the soaps shown in this section are uncolored and generally unscented, you can easily incorporate your favorite natural colorants (see pages 145 to 154), essential oil blends (pages 155 to 160), herbal infusions (pages 162 to 166) or special additives (pages 161 to 162) into the recipes without needing to change lye or oil amounts. Feel free to personalize these recipes any way you like!

Easiest Ever Castile Soap

Classic castile soap is made with 100 percent pure olive oil. Because of the high amount of olive oil, it requires a longer cure time than many other types of soap, but the long wait is well worth it. The extra cure time results in a harder long-lasting bar of soap that has little lather, but is ideally suited for cleansing the most sensitive skin types. Some people adore the mildness of castile, while others are not a fan of its lack of noticeable bubbles. In this recipe, I chose to add a blend of relaxing lavender and lemony litsea essential oils for scent, but you can substitute other essential oils (see page 155 for ideas) or omit them completely for an unscented bar. Because castile soap needs such a long cure time, I recommend adding rosemary antioxidants (also called ROE, or rosemary oleoresin extract) to ensure a satisfactory shelf life. (See page 17 for more on extending the shelf life of soaps.)

YIELD: 7 TO 8 BARS OF SOAP (2.5 LBS/1.13 KG)

7.5 oz (213 g) distilled water

3.6 oz (102 g) sodium hydroxide (lye)

28 oz (794 g) olive oil (100%)

0.7 oz (20 g) lavender essential oil (optional)

0.53 oz (15 g) litsea essential oil (optional)

0.04 oz (1 g) rosemary antioxidants (optional)

Wearing protective gloves and eyewear, carefully stir the lye into the distilled water. Please note that this recipe has a fairly significant water discount. That means that it has less water than normal to offset castile soap's tendency to take a long time to reach trace and release from a mold. Set the lye solution aside in a safe place to cool for about 30 to 40 minutes or until the temperature drops to around 100 to 110°F (38 to 43°C). Warm the olive oil to around 100 to 110°F (38 to 43°C), then combine it with the cooled lye solution. Using a combination of hand stirring and an immersion blender, stir the soap until it reaches trace.

At trace, hand-stir in the essential oils, if using, then pour into a prepared mold. Cover lightly with a sheet of wax or freezer paper, then a towel or light blanket. Peek at the soap every so often; if it starts developing a crack, move it to a cooler location. Keep the soap in the mold for 2 to 3 days, or until it's easy to remove, then slice into bars when it's firm enough not to stick to your cutting tool. Cure on coated cooling racks or sheets of wax paper for at least 6 to 8 weeks before using. Ideally, castile soap should cure even longer, at least 4 to 6 months.

TIP: To slightly increase the bubble factor in low lathering soaps like castile, try dissolving 1 teaspoon (4 g) granulated sugar in 1 tablespoon (15 ml) distilled water for every pound of oils in your recipe. In this recipe, that equals 1³/₄ teaspoons (7.3 g) sugar and 1³/₄ tablespoons (26 ml) of water. Thoroughly stir the sugar solution into the soap batter before adding essential oils.

Beginner's Bastille Soap

Bastille soap is similar to castile, only instead of using 100 percent olive oil, you incorporate another oil or two in the recipe to help improve lather or add other desirable qualities to the finished bar. In this recipe, I chose to include coconut oil for its additional cleansing and lathering properties. The classic fragrance of lavender essential oil adds a lovely light aroma to the finished soap, but you can choose another type if you wish (see page 155 for more on essential oils), or leave it out completely for an unscented soap.

YIELD: 7 TO 8 BARS OF SOAP (2.5 LBS/1.13 KG)

8 oz (227 g) distilled water

3.8 oz (108 g) sodium hydroxide (lye)

5 oz (142 g) coconut oil (18%)

23 oz (652 g) olive oil (82%)

1.23 oz (35 g) lavender essential oil (optional)

Wearing protective gloves and eyewear, carefully stir the lye into the distilled water. Please note that this recipe has a slightly higher water discount than many of the other recipes in this book. That means that it has less water than normal to offset bastille soap's tendency to take a longer time to reach trace and release from a mold. Set the lye solution aside in a safe place to cool for about 30 to 40 minutes or until the temperature drops to around 100 to 110°F (38 to 43°C). Melt the coconut oil, then add it to the olive oil. Combine the warm oils and the cooled lye solution. Using a combination of hand stirring and an immersion blender, stir the soap until it reaches trace.

At trace, hand-stir in the essential oil, if using, then pour into a prepared mold. Cover lightly with a sheet of wax or freezer paper, then a towel or light blanket. Peek at the soap every so often; if it starts developing a crack, move it to a cooler location. Keep the soap in the mold for 2 to 3 days, or until it's easy to remove, then slice into bars when it's firm enough not to stick to your cutting tool. Cure on coated cooling racks or sheets of wax paper for at least 6 weeks before using.

TIP: You can enrich almost any soap recipe in this book, including this one, by adding 1 tablespoon (about 7 g) of powdered goat, cow or coconut milk. Simply use an immersion blender to thoroughly blend the powder into the oils before combining with the cooled lye solution. The natural sugars in milk powder help to boost lather and give a creamier feel to soap. (See page 166 for more ways to add milk to soap recipes.)

SUBSTITUTION: If you're allergic to coconut oil, try using babassu oil in its place. The lye amount will change slightly to 3.76 ounces (106 g).

Creamy Shea Butter Bastille Soap

Like the Beginner's Bastille Soap recipe on page 30, this skin nourishing soap contains a high amount of olive oil. The recipe also includes shea butter for its fantastic ability to condition and moisturize skin, along with castor oil, which helps boost lather. I left this batch unscented, but you may wish to stir in an essential oil or blend at light trace. (See page 155 for more on adding essential oils to your soap recipes.)

YIELD: 7 TO 8 BARS OF SOAP (2.5 LBS/1.13 KG)

8 oz (227 g) distilled water

3.55 oz (101 g) sodium hydroxide (lye)

21 oz (595 g) olive oil (75%)

4.5 oz (128 g) shea butter (16%)

2.5 oz (71 g) castor oil (9%)

Wearing protective gloves and eyewear, carefully stir the lye into the distilled water. Please note that this recipe has a slightly higher water discount than many of the other recipes in this book. That means that it has less water than normal to offset bastille soap's tendency to take a longer time to reach trace and release from a mold. Set the lye solution aside in a safe place to cool for about 30 to 40 minutes or until the temperature drops to around 100 to 110°F (38 to 43°C). Melt the shea butter and add to the other oils. Combine the warmed oils and the cooled lye solution. Using a combination of hand stirring and an immersion blender, stir the soap until it reaches trace.

At trace, pour into a prepared mold or individual molds. Cover lightly with a sheet of wax or freezer paper, then a towel or light blanket. Peek at the soap every so often; if it starts developing a crack, move it to a cooler location. Keep the soap in the mold for 2 to 3 days, or until it's easy to remove, then slice it into bars when it's firm enough not to stick to your cutting tool. Cure on coated cooling racks or sheets of wax paper for at least 6 weeks before using.

SUBSTITUTION: If shea butter isn't available or you're allergic, try substituting with mango butter, cocoa butter, lard or tallow. The lye amount will still fall within acceptable levels with any of these changes, so it will not need to be adjusted.

Pure Coconut Oil Bars

Coconut oil offers a tremendous amount of lather and hardness to a recipe, but it's also highly cleansing. When used at 100 percent in soap, it can leave your skin overly dry unless you also incorporate a high superfat, such as the 20 percent used in this recipe. (See page 18 for more information about superfat levels in soap.) For an added hint of natural color and potential skin benefits, try infusing the coconut oil with herbal flowers such as calendula, dandelion or chamomile first. (See page 162 for how to create herbal oil infusions.)

YIELD: 7 TO 8 BARS OF SOAP (2.5 LBS/1.13 KG)

8.75 oz (248 g) distilled water

4.10 oz (116 g) sodium hydroxide (lye)

28 oz (794 g) coconut oil (100%)

Wearing protective gloves and eyewear, carefully stir the lye into the distilled water. Set the lye solution aside in a safe place to cool for about 30 to 40 minutes or until the temperature drops to around 100 to 110°F (38 to 43°C). Melt the coconut oil, then combine with the cooled lye solution. Using a combination of hand stirring and an immersion blender, stir the soap until it reaches trace.

At trace, pour into a prepared mold. Cover lightly with a sheet of wax or freezer paper, then a towel or light blanket. Peek at the soap every so often; if it starts developing a crack, move it to a cooler location. Keep the soap in the mold for 24 hours or until it's easy to remove. Pure coconut oil soap hardens quickly, so it's best to slice it into bars soon after making or use individual molds. Cure on coated cooling racks or sheets of wax paper about 4 weeks before using.

TIP: This same recipe can be used as laundry soap by keeping the amount of coconut oil the same, but increasing the amount of lye to 5.15 ounces (146 g), reducing the superfat to zero percent. It will be too drying to use on your skin with that adjustment, but makes a wonderful stain stick or ingredient in homemade laundry detergent recipes.

Old-Fashioned Lye Soap

This homey old-fashioned soap is made from 100 percent lard, with an alternate option for those who wish to use tallow instead. (For a vegan alternative, check out Pure Coconut Oil Bars on page 34.) Old-fashioned lye soap has a low creamy lather and is a classic remedy for skin irritations such as poison oak or ivy. I added a combination of lavender and tea tree essential oil for a classic clean scent, but you may wish to leave the soap completely unscented or try an alternate blend suggestion on page 155.

YIELD: 7 TO 8 BARS OF SOAP (2.5 LBS/1.13 KG)

8.75 oz (248 g) distilled water

3.65 oz (103 g) sodium hydroxide (lye)

28 oz (794 g) lard (100%)

0.88 oz (25 g) lavender essential oil (optional)

0.28 oz (8 g) tea tree essential oil (optional)

Wearing protective gloves and eyewear, carefully stir the lye into the distilled water. Set the lye solution aside in a safe place to cool for about 30 to 40 minutes or until the temperature drops to around 100 to 110°F (38 to 43°C). Melt the lard, then combine with the cooled lye solution. Using a combination of hand stirring and an immersion blender, stir the soap until it reaches trace.

At trace, stir in the essential oils, if using. Pour the soap batter into a prepared mold. Cover lightly with a sheet of wax or freezer paper, then a towel or light blanket. Peek at the soap every so often; if it starts developing a crack, move it to a cooler location. Keep the soap in the mold for 1 to 2 days, or until it's easy to remove, then slice it into bars when it's firm enough not to stick to your cutting tool. Cure on coated cooling racks or sheets of wax paper about 4 weeks before using.

SUBSTITUTION: If you want to use tallow instead of lard, slightly adjust the lye amount to 3.7 ounces (105 g).

TIP: If you want to make a pure lard or tallow soap with milk, see page 166 for how to add milk to soap recipes.

Basic Palm-Free Soap Recipes (3 Customizable Versions)

Each of these basic recipes can be used as a blank canvas of sorts to design your own unique soap creations. You can choose to leave the soap plain and unscented, or add a natural colorant (see pages 145 to 154), an essential oil (see pages 155 to 160), herbal infusion (see page 162) or additives of your choice, such as honey and oatmeal (see page 161). Choices for the liquid portion include distilled water, aloe vera liquid, cold coffee, milk (see page 166) or herbal tea (see page 165). Following these formulas, there's no end to the creative combinations you can make!

YIELD: 7 TO 8 BARS OF SOAP (2.5 LBS/1.13 KG)

PALM-FREE SOAP #1: TALLOW/LARD VERSION

8.75 oz (248 g) distilled water or liquid of choice

3.9 oz (111 g) sodium hydroxide (lye)

6.5 oz (184 g) coconut oil (23.2%)

4 oz (113 g) lard or tallow (14.3%)

12 oz (340 g) olive oil (42.9%)

2 oz (57 g) castor oil (7.1%)

3.5 oz (99 g) sunflower or sweet almond oil (12.5%)

1.06 to 1.23 oz (30 to 35 g) essential oil of your choice (optional)

Natural colorant of your choice (optional)

PALM-FREE SOAP #2: VEGAN, WITH BUTTERS

8.75 oz (248 g) distilled water or liquid of choice

3.85 oz (109 g) sodium hydroxide (lye)

6.5 oz (184 g) coconut oil (23.2%)

4 oz (113 g) kokum or cocoa butter (14.3%)

12 oz (340 g) olive oil (42.9%)

2 oz (57 g) castor oil (7.1%)

3.5 oz (99 g) sunflower or sweet almond oil (12.5%)

1.06 to 1.23 oz (30 to 35 g) essential oil of your choice (optional)

Natural colorant of your choice (optional)

PALM-FREE SOAP #3: VEGAN, NO BUTTERS

8.75 oz (248 g) distilled water or liquid of choice

3.95 oz (112 g) sodium hydroxide (lye)

8 oz (227 g) coconut oil (28.6%)

14 oz (397 g) olive oil (50%)

4 oz (113 g) sunflower or sweet almond oil (14.3%)

2 oz (57 g) castor oil (7.1%)

1.06 to 1.23 oz (30 to 35 g) essential oil of your choice (optional)

Natural colorant of your choice (optional)

Wearing protective gloves and eyewear, carefully stir the lye into the distilled water or liquid of choice. Set the lye solution aside in a safe place to cool for about 30 to 40 minutes or until the temperature drops to around 100 to 110°F (38 to 43°C). Melt the coconut oil and other solid fats (such as lard, tallow, kokum or cocoa butter), then add to the other oils. Combine the cooled lye solution with the warm oils. Using a combination of hand stirring and an immersion blender, stir the soap until it reaches trace.

At trace, add essential oils, if using. Pour into a prepared mold. Cover lightly with a sheet of wax or freezer paper, then a towel or light blanket. Peek at the soap every so often; if it starts developing a crack, move it to a cooler location. Keep the soap in the mold for 1 to 2 days, or until it's easy to remove, then slice it into bars when it's firm enough not to stick to your cutting tool. Cure on coated cooling racks or sheets of wax paper about 4 weeks before using.

*See photo on page 26.

> TIP: These recipes, along with many in the book, have a built-in water discount to ensure that the resulting soaps release more easily from their molds. (Without the hardening properties of palm oil, palm-free soaps tend to start off softer but will further harden over cure time.) If you find that your soaps reach trace too quickly, add an additional 0.5 ounces (14 g) of distilled water to the recipe.

Soaps from the
Herb Garden

Herbs and flowers provide an abundant source of inspiration and ingredients for the creative natural soapmaker.

Oils and teas enriched with beloved skin-care herbs such as chamomile, roses and comfrey are easy to work into any soap recipe (see pages 155 to 166 for more on herbal teas and oil infusions). Anecdotal evidence from veteran soapmakers, combined with years of my own experience and the fact that many beneficial herbal constituents are resistant to both lye and heat, makes it reasonable to assume that soaps containing herbs can offer additional skin benefits in many cases. (This book was written for beginner and hobbyist soapmakers, so if you plan to sell your soaps one day, be sure to research labeling laws and not make herbal health claims relating to your soap.)

Refreshing mint, lovely roses and the spicy sweet purple basil growing in my gardens helped inspire recipes such as Double Mint Tiger Stripe Soap (page 44), Purple Basil & Mint Layers (page 51) and Grandma's Yellow Roses Soap (page 47).

Humble and often undervalued, weeds such as plantain, violets and dandelions are some of the best skin-soothers around. (See page 162 to find more herbs that are good for your skin.) After trying a batch of Sunny Dandelion Oatmeal Soap (page 52) or Weedy Greens Jewelweed & Plantain Bars (page 55), I think you'll be a fan of them as well!

Lavender Chamomile Shampoo & Body Bars

These bars feature a double dose of scalp-soothing chamomile, incorporating both a tea and oil infusion of the flowers. If chamomile isn't available, try using calendula or dandelion flowers instead. A generous amount of castor oil, combined with the natural sugars in honey, ensures a terrific lathering experience. Lavender essential oil not only contributes a subtle stress-reducing scent, but is purported to help promote hair growth as well. Don't feel limited to using shampoo bars only on your hair; they make an excellent body or hand soap too!

YIELD: 7 TO 8 BARS OF SOAP (2.5 LBS/1.13 KG)

8.75 oz (248 g) cold chamomile tea (see page 165 for how to make herbal tea)

3.9 oz (111 g) sodium hydroxide (lye)

8 oz (227 g) coconut oil (28.6%)

2 oz (57 g) shea butter (7.1%)

10 oz (283 g) chamomile-infused olive oil (see page 155 for how to infuse oils) (35.7%)

4 oz (113 g) castor oil (14.3%)

4 oz (113 g) sweet almond or sunflower oil (14.3%)

1.23 oz (35 g) lavender essential oil

1 tsp (5 ml) honey diluted with 1 tsp (5 ml) water

Wearing protective gloves and eyewear, carefully stir the lye into the cool chamomile tea. It's normal for the lye solution to turn a golden brown at this point. Set the lye solution aside in a safe place to cool for about 30 to 40 minutes or until the temperature drops to around 100 to 110°F (38 to 43°C). Warm the oils to around 100 to 110°F (38 to 43°C), then combine with the cooled lye solution. Using a combination of hand stirring and an immersion blender, stir the soap until it reaches trace.

At trace, hand-stir in the lavender essential oil and diluted honey, then pour into a prepared mold. Cover lightly with a sheet of wax or freezer paper, then a towel or light blanket. Peek at the soap every so often; if it starts developing a crack, move it to a cooler location. Keep the soap in the mold for 1 to 2 days, then remove and slice it into bars when it's firm enough not to stick to your cutting tool. Cure on coated cooling racks or sheets of wax paper about 4 weeks before using.

SUBSTITUTION: To replace shea butter, try using mango, cocoa or kokum butter, or lard or tallow instead. The lye amount will stay within an acceptable range for each of these changes so will not need to be adjusted.

Double Mint Tiger Stripe Soap

A combination of peppermint and spearmint essential oils adds a delightful and uplifting scent to this refreshing soap. A simple tiger stripe, colored with French green clay and indigo, runs throughout each bar, but you could also add the colorants to the entire batch for a single-colored soap or leave it out entirely if you wish. White kaolin clay is added to the lye water to brighten and lighten the overall soap color, allowing the natural shades of the colorants to shine through.

YIELD: 7 TO 8 BARS OF SOAP (2.5 LBS/1.13 KG)

9 oz (255 g) distilled water

3.9 oz (111 g) sodium hydroxide (lye)

1 tbsp (6 g) white kaolin clay powder

4 oz (113 g) cocoa or kokum butter (14%)

7.5 oz (213 g) coconut oil (27%)

10.5 oz (298 g) olive oil (37.5%)

1.5 oz (43 g) castor oil (5.5%)

4.5 oz (128 g) rice bran oil (16%)

0.53 oz (15 g) peppermint essential oil

0.53 oz (15 g) spearmint essential oil

2 tsp (4g) French green clay + ¼ tsp indigo powder, mixed with 4 tsp (20 ml) hot water

Wearing protective gloves and eyewear, carefully stir the lye into the distilled water. Stir in the kaolin clay powder until dissolved. Set the lye solution aside in a safe place to cool for about 30 to 40 minutes or until the temperature drops to around 100 to 110°F (38 to 43°C). Melt the cocoa butter and coconut oil then add to the other oils. Combine the warmed oils with the cooled lye solution. Using a combination of hand stirring and an immersion blender, stir the soap until it reaches light trace. Be sure not to make the soap batter too thick if you're planning to do the tiger stripe design.

At light trace, stir in the essential oils by hand. Working quickly but carefully, weigh out half of the soap batter, or around 22 ounces (624 g), into a separate container. In that portion, stir in the French green clay and indigo mixture until it's thoroughly incorporated. Leave the remainder of the soap batter plain white.

Using the instructions on page 174 if needed, alternate pouring the two soap batters in single straight lines down the center of the mold. Cover lightly with a sheet of wax or freezer paper, then a towel or light blanket. Peek at the soap every so often; if it starts developing a crack, move it to a cooler location. Keep the soap in the mold for 1 to 2 days, or until it's easy to remove, then slice it into bars when it's firm enough not to stick to your cutting tool. Cure on coated cooling racks or sheets of wax paper about 4 weeks before using.

SUBSTITUTION: If castor oil is unavailable, you can use more olive oil in its place, keeping in mind that castor oil helps boost lather while olive oil does not, so your soap will be less bubbly. The lye amount will stay within an acceptable range and will not need to be adjusted.

Cocoa or kokum butter can be replaced in equal measure with lard or tallow, without needing to adjust lye amount.

Grandma's Yellow Roses Soap

This sweet old-fashioned rose soap was made using a silicone mold imprinted with a rose pattern, but it can just as easily be made in a loaf mold and sliced into standard bars. Lemon peel powder gives a subtle yellow tint to the finished soap, but you can use annatto seed or saffron powder (see page 145) for a brighter shade of yellow. I like to use rose-infused olive oil (see page 162 for how to make it) in rose-themed soaps like this one, but you can use plain olive oil instead. Tallow's main purpose in the recipe is to provide an alternative to the hardness that palm oil normally provides, but for a vegan alternative, check out the substitution tips below.

YIELD: 7 TO 8 BARS OF SOAP (2.5 LBS/1.13 KG)

8.75 oz (248 g) distilled water

3.95 oz (112 g) sodium hydroxide (lye)

1½ tsp (5 g) lemon peel powder

7.5 oz (213 g) coconut oil (26.8%)

4 oz (113 g) tallow or lard (14.3%)

12 oz (340 g) olive oil (42.8%)

4 oz (113 g) sunflower or sweet almond oil (14.3%)

0.5 oz (14 g) rosehip seed oil (1.8%)

0.88 oz (25 g) geranium essential oil

0.35 oz (10 g) lavender essential oil

Wearing protective gloves and eyewear, carefully stir the lye into the distilled water. Add the lemon peel powder to the lye solution. Set the lye solution aside in a safe place to cool for about 30 to 40 minutes or until the temperature drops to around 100 to 110°F (38 to 43°C). Melt the coconut oil and tallow, then add to the other oils. Combine the warm oils with the cooled lye solution. Using a combination of hand stirring and an immersion blender, stir the soap until it reaches light trace.

At trace, stir in the essential oils, then pour into a prepared mold. Cover lightly with a sheet of wax or freezer paper, then a towel or light blanket. Peek at the soap every so often; if it starts developing a crack, move it to a cooler location. Keep the soap in the mold for 1 to 2 days, or until it's easy to remove, then slice it into bars when it's firm enough not to stick to your cutting tool. Cure on coated cooling racks or sheets of wax paper about 4 weeks before using.

SUBSTITUTION: Tallow or lard can be replaced in equal measure with cocoa or kokum butter, without needing to adjust lye amount. If rosehip seed oil isn't available, try using sweet almond or more olive oil in its place.

Soothing Comfrey & Aloe Soap

Twice the herbal goodness can be found in this skin-soothing soap. Comfrey is a natural source of allantoin, an ingredient used in skin care products for its anti-inflammatory and skin regenerating effects. Aloe vera liquid is a thin water-like aloe extract sold by soap supply companies or possibly your local health store. It's used to cool and relieve itchy irritated skin and make soap extra bubbly and moisturizing. This recipe requires a small amount of preparation the day before you plan on making the soap, or you could use a pre-made herbal infusion instead. (See page 162 for how to make herbal-infused oils.) Look for a deep green unrefined hempseed oil and it will give your soap a lovely shade of natural green along with a generous dose of beneficial essential fatty acids.

YIELD: 7 TO 8 BARS OF SOAP (2.5 LBS/1.13 KG)

1 tbsp (2.3 g) dried comfrey leaf

12 oz (340 g) olive oil (42.5%)

8.75 oz (248 g) aloe vera liquid

3.9 oz (111 g) sodium hydroxide (lye)

8 oz (227 g) coconut oil (28.5%)

4 oz (113 g) shea butter (14.5%)

4 oz (113 g) unrefined hempseed oil (14.5%)

SUBSTITUTION: To replace shea butter, try using kokum, mango or cocoa butter, or lard or tallow instead. The lye amount does not need to be changed.

Hempseed oil can be replaced with avocado oil, with no lye adjustment required.

FOR THE COMFREY-INFUSED OIL

Place the dried comfrey leaf in a heatproof jar and cover with the olive oil. Set the jar down into a small saucepan containing a few inches of water, forming a makeshift double boiler. Heat over a low burner for around 2 hours. Remove from the heat and allow the oil to continue infusing overnight. Strain through a stainless steel strainer before using in the recipe, adding additional olive oil as needed so the total amount of olive oil used in the recipe is exactly 12 ounces (340 g).

FOR THE COMFREY AND ALOE SOAP

Wearing protective gloves and eyewear, carefully stir the lye into the liquid aloe vera. It's normal for the lye solution to turn a golden-green color. Set the lye solution aside in a safe place to cool for about 30 to 40 minutes or until the temperature drops to around 100 to 110°F (38 to 43°C). Melt the shea butter and coconut oil, then add them to the remaining oils. The oil mixture will be a dark green color from the comfrey-infused olive and hempseed oils. Combine the warm oils with the cooled lye solution. Using a combination of hand stirring and an immersion blender, stir the soap until it reaches light trace.

Pour the soap batter into a prepared mold. Cover lightly with a sheet of wax or freezer paper, then a towel or light blanket. Peek at the soap every so often; if it starts developing a crack, move it to a cooler location. Keep the soap in the mold for 1 to 2 days, then remove and slice it into bars when it's firm enough not to stick to your cutting tool. Cure on coated cooling racks or sheets of wax paper about 4 weeks before using.

Purple Basil & Mint Layers Soap

Basil contains notable antioxidant, anti-inflammatory and anti-aging properties, making it a useful addition to soaps and skin care products. While this recipe features fresh purple basil leaves, you could use green basil or even fresh mint leaves in the green portion of the soap instead. If basil isn't available or in season where you live, try making the soap with plain distilled water or a light-colored herbal tea in its place. Kokum butter helps provide some of the hardness often lacking in palm-free soaps, but it can be replaced with tallow or lard, following the substitution tips below.

YIELD: 7 TO 8 BARS OF SOAP (2.5 LBS/1.13 KG)

$1/2$ cup (15 g) fresh purple basil leaves

2 tbsp (30 ml) distilled water

1 tsp (3.6 g) purple Brazilian clay

2 tsp (9.5 g) French green clay mixed with 2 tbsp (30 ml) distilled water

8.75 oz (248 g) distilled water

3.9 oz (111 g) sodium hydroxide (lye)

7 oz (198 g) coconut oil (25%)

4.5 oz (128 g) kokum butter (16%)

12 oz (340 g) olive oil (43%)

4.5 oz (128 g) sunflower or sweet almond oil (16%)

0.88 oz (25 g) peppermint essential oil

0.14 oz (4 g) basil essential oil (about $1^{1}/_8$ tsp)

SUBSTITUTION: Kokum butter can be replaced in equal measure with cocoa butter, tallow or lard, without needing to adjust lye amount.

If you're allergic to coconut oil, try using babassu oil instead. The lye amount will need to be adjusted slightly lower, to 3.85 ounces (109 g).

TO PREPARE THE NATURAL COLORANTS

Blend the fresh basil leaves with the 2 tablespoons (30 ml) of distilled water in a blender or food processor until fully pureed. Strain using a fine stainless steel strainer. Make sure that the resulting juice isn't too darkly colored as it will carry through to your final soap and muddy the purple clay. If needed, add extra water to lighten the color some. Mix $1^1/_2$ tablespoons (22 ml) of the resulting basil juice with the purple Brazilian clay. Set aside with the French green clay and water mixture, until needed.

FOR THE BASIL AND MINT SOAP

Wearing protective gloves and eyewear, carefully stir the lye into the distilled water. Set the lye solution aside in a safe place to cool for about 30 to 40 minutes or until the temperature drops to around 100 to 110°F (38 to 43°C). Melt the kokum butter and coconut oil, then add them to the remaining oils. Combine the warm oils with the cooled lye solution. Using a combination of hand stirring and an immersion blender, stir the soap until it reaches a very light trace.

Add the essential oils. Divide the soap batter equally into two containers. In one container of soap batter, stir in the purple clay and basil juice mixture until well blended. In the second container of soap batter, thoroughly stir in the French green clay mixture.

Following the directions for creating simple layers on page 170, pour the green soap batter into the bottom of a prepared mold. Next, pour the purple layer of soap. If desired, texturize the top of the soap. (See page 168 for tips on adding texture to soap tops.)

Cover lightly with a sheet of wax or freezer paper, then a towel or light blanket. Peek at the soap every so often; if it starts developing a crack, move it to a cooler location. Keep the soap in the mold for 1 to 2 days, then remove and slice it into bars when it's firm enough not to stick to your cutting tool. Cure on coated cooling racks or sheets of wax paper about 4 weeks before using.

Sunny Dandelion Oatmeal Soap

Lecithin-rich dandelion flowers pair up with skin-soothing oats to make a soap that's perfectly suited for itchy or sensitive skin. Pre-infusing the olive oil with dandelion flowers also turns the soap a subtle shade of pale yellow that will stick around for a few months before fading to off-white. Castor oil was added to improve lather, while sweet almond oil nourishes your skin. Cocoa butter contributes additional hardness to the finished bars, but if you're allergic, see the substitution tip for an alternative. A bright blend of orange and bergamot essential oils gives this soap a lively scent, but they can easily be omitted or substituted for the essential oil of your choice. If dandelions aren't in season, this recipe is equally lovely when calendula or chamomile flowers are used instead.

YIELD: 7 TO 8 BARS OF SOAP (2.5 LBS/1.13 KG)

8.75 oz (248 g) distilled water

3.9 oz (111 g) sodium hydroxide (lye)

7.5 oz (213 g) coconut oil (26.8%)

3.5 oz (99 g) cocoa butter (12.5%)

11.5 oz (326 g) dandelion-infused olive oil (see page 162 for how to infuse oils) (41%)

3.5 oz (99 g) sweet almond or sunflower oil (12.5%)

2 oz (57 g) castor oil (7.1%)

0.7 oz (20 g) orange essential oil (use a folded or Valencia type) (optional)

0.53 oz (15 g) bergamot essential oil (optional)

1 tbsp (7 g) rolled oats, ground very fine to powder

1 tsp (5 ml) honey diluted with 1 tsp (5 ml) water (optional)

Wearing protective gloves and eyewear, carefully stir the lye into the distilled water. Set the lye solution aside in a safe place to cool for about 30 to 40 minutes or until the temperature drops to around 100 to 110°F (38 to 43°C). Warm the oils to 100 to 110°F (38 to 43°C), then combine with the cooled lye solution. Using a combination of hand stirring and an immersion blender, stir the soap until it reaches trace.

At trace, hand stir in the powdered oats, diluted honey and essential oils, if using, then pour into a prepared mold. Cover lightly with a sheet of freezer or wax paper, then a towel or light blanket. Peek at the soap every so often; if it starts developing a crack, move it to a cooler location. Keep the soap in the mold for 1 to 2 days, then remove and slice it into bars when it's firm enough not to stick to your cutting tool. Cure on coated wire cooling racks or sheets of wax paper about 4 weeks before using.

SUBSTITUTION: If castor oil is unavailable, you can use more olive oil in its place, keeping in mind that castor oil helps boost lather while olive oil does not, so your soap will be less bubbly. The lye amount will stay within an acceptable range and will not need to be adjusted.

Cocoa butter can be replaced in equal measure with kokum butter, tallow or lard, without needing to adjust the lye amount.

For vegan soap, omit the honey or replace it with agave syrup.

Weedy Greens Jewelweed & Plantain Soap

Plantain is a common leafy green weed found throughout much of the world that soothes, cools and moisturizes. Jewelweed, also called touch-me-not, is a weed with pretty orange flowers that grows around moist areas. It's especially prized for its ability to soothe the pain and irritation of poison ivy and other such maladies. If plantain and jewelweed aren't available where you live, you can substitute with viola leaves, chickweed and/or comfrey leaves. Be aware that the green color of chlorella fades after several months. For a longer lasting green, you could consider using French green clay (see page 145) in place of, or in combination with, the chlorella.

YIELD: 7 TO 8 BARS OF SOAP (2.5 LBS/1.13 KG)

1 cup (35 g) chopped fresh jewelweed flowers & leaves

1 cup (35 g) chopped fresh plantain leaves

8.75 oz (248 g) distilled water

3.95 oz (112 g) sodium hydroxide (lye)

1 tsp (4 g) chlorella powder

8 oz (227 g) coconut oil (28.5%)

12 oz (340 g) olive oil (43%)

4 oz (113 g) rice bran oil (14.25%)

4 oz (113 g) sunflower or sweet almond oil (14.25%)

1.06 oz (30 g) lavender essential oil (optional)

TIP: If fresh herbs aren't available, you can use dried herbs to make an herbal tea infusion instead. Chill and measure out 8.75 ounces (248 g) of cold herbal tea to use in the recipe. (See page 165 for more on making tea infusions.)

FOR THE JEWELWEED AND PLANTAIN JUICE

Thoroughly blend fresh plantain and jewelweed together with 2 ounces (57 g) of water in a blender or food processor until fully pureed. Add the rest of the distilled water and stir well. Place the mixture in a refrigerator to infuse for several hours or overnight. Remove and strain the resulting greenish-brown juice. Weigh out 8.5 ounces (241 g) for use in the soap recipe, adding more plain distilled water if needed.

FOR THE JEWELWEED AND PLANTAIN SOAP

Wearing protective gloves and eyewear, carefully stir the lye into the chilled plantain and jewelweed juice. Stir in the chlorella powder. The lye solution may develop an unpleasant, almost skunk-like smell. That's a completely normal, but temporary, condition when working with jewelweed. Set the lye solution aside in a safe place to cool for about 30 to 40 minutes or until the temperature drops to around 100 to 110°F (38 to 43°C). Warm the oils to 100 to 110°F (38 to 43°C), then combine with the cooled lye solution. Using a combination of hand stirring and an immersion blender, stir the soap until it reaches trace.

At trace, stir in the lavender essential oil, if using, then pour into a prepared mold or individual molds. Cover lightly with a sheet of freezer or wax paper, then a towel or light blanket. Peek at the soap every so often; if it starts developing a crack, move it to a cooler location. Keep the soap in the mold for 1 to 2 days, then remove and slice it into bars when it's firm enough not to stick to your cutting tool. Cure on coated wire cooling racks or sheets of wax paper about 4 weeks before using.

SUBSTITUTION: The rice bran oil can be replaced with more olive oil, without the need to adjust the lye amount. If you're allergic to coconut oil, use an equal amount of babassu oil instead. The lye amount will change slightly, to 3.85 ounces (109 g).

Chamomile Tallow Bars

Reminiscent of an early summer garden, this soap is primarily scented with geranium essential oil for a lovely rose-like scent. The inclusion of tallow contributes to a harder, long lasting bar of soap with a great lather, but an alternative is given if you're looking for a vegan option instead. Nourishing apricot kernel oil adds a touch of luxury to the finished bars, but if you're not able to obtain any, try substituting with sweet almond or sunflower oil instead.

YIELD: 7 TO 8 BARS OF SOAP (2.5 LBS/1.13 KG)

8.75 oz (248 g) distilled water

3.9 oz (111 g) sodium hydroxide (lye)

12 oz (340 g) chamomile-infused olive oil (see page 162 for how to infuse oils) (42.9%)

5.5 oz (156 g) tallow (or lard) (19.6%)

7 oz (198 g) coconut oil (25%)

3.5 oz (99 g) apricot kernel oil (12.5%)

0.70 oz (20 g) geranium essential oil

0.35 oz (10 g) litsea essential oil

0.28 oz (8 g) grapefruit essential oil

Wearing protective gloves and eyewear, carefully stir the lye into the distilled water. Set the lye solution aside in a safe place to cool for about 30 to 40 minutes or until the temperature drops to around 100 to 110°F (38 to 43°C). Warm the oils to 100 to 110°F (38 to 43°C), then combine with the cooled lye solution. Using a combination of hand stirring and an immersion blender, stir the soap until it reaches trace.

At trace, hand-stir in the essential oils, then pour into a prepared mold. Cover lightly with a sheet of wax or freezer paper, then a towel or light blanket. Peek at the soap every so often; if it starts developing a crack, move it to a cooler location. Keep the soap in the mold for 1 to 2 days, then remove and slice it into bars when it's firm enough not to stick to your cutting tool. Cure on coated cooling racks or sheets of wax paper about 4 weeks before using.

SUBSTITUTION: For a vegan option, omit the 5.5 ounces (156 g) of tallow. Replace with 4 ounces (113 g) of cocoa butter plus 1.5 ounces (43 g) of castor oil to make up the balance. The lye amount will remain unchanged.

Soaps from the Orchard & Veggie Garden

Gathered from your backyard or local farmers' market, fresh produce offers a creative means to enrich your soaps with extra nutrients and an added fun factor.

The alkaline nature of soap keeps it from spoiling easily, even when food purees are incorporated, so you don't have to worry about a shorter shelf life with these kinds of soaps.

Have an abundance of lycopene-rich tomatoes in your garden this year? Try your hand at a batch of Heirloom Tomato Soap (page 68). If you're a fan of the classics, you're sure to love gentle Simply Carrot Soap (page 64) or soothing Pumpkin Oatmeal Soap (page 60).

Dry or sensitive skin types won't want to miss experiencing extra-rich Creamy Avocado Soap (page 67) or Fresh Aloe & Cucumber Soap (page 71).

Pumpkin Oatmeal Soap

Loaded with vitamin A and other powerhouse nutrients, real pumpkin puree gives soap a natural hint of yellow-orange color. Ground oats help soothe irritations or itchiness, while honey boosts bubbles and adds extra nourishment. Cocoa butter not only protects skin, but also results in a harder bar of soap. Both almond and sunflower oil work equally well in this recipe to help nourish and condition. I left this soap unscented so it would be suitable for sensitive skin types, but you could also choose to add essential oils for natural fragrance. (See page 155 for essential oil and blend ideas.)

YIELD: 7 TO 8 BARS OF SOAP (2.5 LBS/1.13 KG)

6.5 oz (184 g) distilled water

3.9 oz (111 g) sodium hydroxide (lye)

2.5 oz (71 g) pumpkin puree

7.5 oz (213 g) coconut oil (26.8%)

4 oz (113 g) cocoa butter (14.3%)

13.5 oz (383 g) olive oil (48.2%)

3 oz (85 g) sweet almond or sunflower oil (10.7%)

1 tbsp (7 g) rolled oats, ground to a very fine powder

1 tsp (5 ml) honey mixed with 1 tsp (5 ml) water

Wearing protective gloves and eyewear, carefully stir the lye into the distilled water. The lye solution will be more concentrated than normal lye solutions to compensate for the added moisture of the pumpkin puree, so be extra sure that the lye is completely dissolved before proceeding. Set the lye solution aside in a safe place to cool for about 30 to 40 minutes or until the temperature drops to around 100 to 110°F (38 to 43°C). Melt the coconut oil and cocoa butter, then add to the other oils. Using the immersion blender, thoroughly blend the pumpkin puree into the warm oils. Combine the pumpkin and oil mixture with the cooled lye solution. Using a combination of hand stirring and an immersion blender, stir the soap until it reaches light trace.

At trace, stir in the ground oats and honey until thoroughly combined. Pour the soap batter into a prepared mold. Cover lightly with a sheet of wax or freezer paper, then a towel or light blanket. The natural sugars found in honey and pumpkin may make the soap heat up more than normal. Peek at the soap every so often; if it starts developing a crack, move it to a cooler location. Keep the soap in the mold for 1 to 2 days, or until it's easy to remove, then slice it into bars when it's firm enough not to stick to your cutting tool. Cure on coated cooling racks or sheets of wax paper about 4 weeks before using.

TIP: Both canned and homemade cooked puree will work well in this recipe. No pumpkin handy? Try butternut squash puree as a replacement.

SUBSTITUTION: Instead of cocoa butter, try an equal amount of kokum butter, tallow or lard. The lye amount will remain unchanged.

Warm Apple Spice & Ginger Soap

The subtle spicy scent of this soap conjures up images of beautiful fall days and seasonal trips to the apple orchard. Rich in nourishing antioxidants and skin smoothing fruit acids, freshly pressed apple cider is incorporated into this recipe, but if that's not available, you can substitute regular unsweetened apple juice instead. Ground ginger and cinnamon powder infuses the entire soap, lending color and a warm boost to circulation. Since the apple cider and ground spices don't really contribute scent to the recipe, a blend of essential oils provides a warm festive fragrance. Cinnamon leaf and clove are two essential oils that are well known for causing soap batter to suddenly thicken, so be sure to hand-stir them in at light trace and be ready to pour the soap immediately into the mold once incorporated.

YIELD: 7 TO 8 BARS OF SOAP (2.5 LBS/1.13 KG)

4 oz (113 g) cold apple cider or juice

4.75 oz (135 g) distilled water

3.95 oz (112 g) sodium hydroxide (lye)

½ tsp ground ginger

½ tsp ground cinnamon

2 oz (57 g) shea butter (7%)

8 oz (227 g) coconut oil (28.5%)

3.5 oz (99 g) sunflower or sweet almond oil (12.5%)

14.5 oz (411 g) olive oil (52%)

0.18 oz (5 g) cinnamon leaf essential oil (about 1½ tsp)

0.18 oz (5 g) clove essential oil (about 1½ tsp)

0.11 oz (3 g) orange essential oil (use a folded or Valencia type) (about 1 tsp) (optional)

0.14 oz (4 g) dark patchouli essential oil (about 1⅜ tsp) (optional)

Combine the cold apple cider and distilled water. Wearing protective gloves and eyewear, carefully stir the lye into the diluted cider. Next, stir the ginger and cinnamon powders into the lye solution. Set the lye solution aside in a safe place to cool for about 30 to 40 minutes or until the temperature drops to around 100 to 110°F (38 to 43°C). Melt the shea butter and coconut oil, then add to the other oils. Combine the warm oils with the cooled lye solution. Using a combination of hand stirring and an immersion blender, stir the soap until it reaches light trace.

Stir in the essential oils and pour the soap batter into a prepared mold or individual molds. Cover lightly with a sheet of wax or freezer paper, then a towel or light blanket. The apple cider and spices tend to make this soap heat up more than regular soaps. Peek at the soap every so often; if it starts developing a crack, uncover the mold and move it to a cooler location. Keep the soap in the mold for 1 to 2 days, or until it's easy to remove, then slice it into bars when it's firm enough not to stick to your cutting tool. Cure on coated cooling racks or sheets of wax paper about 4 weeks before using.

TIP: Due to the seasonal and local nature of fresh apple cider, your soap may turn out darker or lighter than mine. For an even lighter brown color, omit or decrease the amount of ground cinnamon. For a pretty pink-toned color, try stirring 3 teaspoons (5 g) of madder root powder into the warmed oils before adding the lye solution.

SUBSTITUTION: To replace shea butter, try using mango, cocoa or kokum butter, or lard or tallow instead. The lye amount will stay within an acceptable range for each of these changes so will not need to be adjusted.

Simply Carrot Soap

Rich in antioxidants and beneficial nutrients, carrots are a popular ingredient in soaps, especially facial bars. In this recipe, a portion of the distilled water is replaced with carrot juice. The high amount of olive oil makes it extra gentle on delicate skin, but also requires a little longer cure time than some of the other soap recipes in this book. You can choose to use either sunflower or sweet almond oil in this recipe as both work well to nourish and condition skin. Since carrot soaps are often used on delicate facial skin, I left this soap unscented, but you can add essential oils if you'd like. (See page 155 for essential oil and blend ideas.)

YIELD: 7 TO 8 BARS OF SOAP (2.5 LBS/1.13 KG)

4.25 oz (120 g) strained, chilled carrot juice

4.5 oz (128 g) distilled water

3.95 oz (112 g) sodium hydroxide (lye)

7.5 oz (213 g) coconut oil (27%)

17 oz (482 g) olive oil (60.5%)

3.5 oz (99 g) sunflower or sweet almond oil (12.5%)

Combine the chilled carrot juice and distilled water. Wearing protective gloves and eyewear, carefully stir the lye into the diluted carrot juice. Set the lye solution aside in a safe place to cool for about 30 to 40 minutes or until the temperature drops to around 100 to 110°F (38 to 43°C). Melt the coconut oil, then add to the other oils. Combine the warm oils with the cooled lye solution. Using a combination of hand stirring and an immersion blender, stir the soap until it reaches light trace.

At trace, pour into a prepared mold. Cover lightly with a sheet of wax or freezer paper, then a towel or light blanket. Peek at the soap every so often; if it starts developing a crack, move it to a cooler location. Keep the soap in the mold for 1 to 2 days, or until it's easy to remove, then slice it into bars when it's firm enough not to stick to your cutting tool. Cure on coated cooling racks or sheets of wax paper for 5 to 6 weeks before using.

SUBSTITUTION: High olive oil soaps such as this one tend to be incredibly gentle, but also have less lather. If you'd like to boost the bubbles in the finished soap, omit 2 ounces (57 g) of the olive oil and replace it with 2 ounces (57 g) of castor oil. This will reduce the amount of olive oil in the recipe down to 15 ounces (425 g), and the lye amount will reduce to 3.9 ounces (111 g).

Creamy Avocado Soap

Loaded with essential fatty acids that are great for your skin, fresh avocado puree partners up with the mild cleansing power of French green clay in this nourishing soap that your skin will absolutely love. Shea butter and avocado oil add extra skin softening compounds while a small amount of castor oil gives this soap a boost of lather. This is one soap recipe that I prefer to prevent from gel phase, to better preserve the green color. After filling with soap batter, simply place the mold in your refrigerator for 24 hours. To avoid the chance of a partial gel (see page 183) in the center of the loaf, you may want to consider using individual molds for this recipe. I often leave this soap unscented, but it's also nice with the suggested optional minty blend listed below.

YIELD: 7 TO 8 BARS OF SOAP (2.5 LBS/1.13 KG)

5.75 oz (163 g) distilled water

3.9 oz (111 g) sodium hydroxide (lye)

2 tsp (9.5 g) French green clay

3 oz (85 g) fresh avocado, mashed

7.5 oz (213 g) coconut oil (26.8%)

3.5 oz (99 g) shea butter (12.5%)

11.5 oz (326 g) olive oil (41%)

4 oz (113 g) avocado oil (14.3%)

1.5 oz (43 g) castor oil (5.4%)

0.56 oz (16 g) peppermint essential oil (optional)

0.35 oz (10 g) fir needle essential oil (optional)

0.14 oz (4 g) rosemary essential oil (about 1¼ tsp) (optional)

Wearing protective gloves and eyewear, carefully stir the lye into the distilled water. Note that the water amount is significantly reduced to accommodate the extra moisture provided by the avocado puree. As a result, the lye solution will be more concentrated than normal, so handle carefully. Add the French green clay and stir until well blended. Set the lye solution aside in a safe place to cool for about 30 to 40 minutes or until the temperature drops to around 100 to 110°F (38 to 43°C). Melt the coconut oil and shea butter, then add to the other oils. Add the mashed avocado to the oils, mixing well with an immersion blender until completely incorporated. Be sure there are no large chunks of avocado left, since they can mold in the finished soap. Combine the avocado and warm oil mixture with the cooled lye solution. Using a combination of hand stirring and an immersion blender, stir the soap until it reaches light trace.

At trace, stir in the essential oils, if using. Pour the soap batter into a prepared mold. To preserve the green color of this soap and prevent browning, pop the filled soap mold in your refrigerator for around 24 hours. Afterward, let the mold sit undisturbed for another 1 to 2 days before removing from the mold. Slice it into bars when it's firm enough not to stick to your cutting tool. Cure on coated cooling racks or sheets of wax paper about 4 weeks before using.

SUBSTITUTION: To replace shea butter, try using mango, cocoa or kokum butter, or lard or tallow instead. The lye amount will stay within an acceptable range for each of these changes so it will not need to be adjusted.

If allergic to coconut oil, try using babassu oil instead. The lye amount will need to be reduced to 3.85 ounces (109 g) with this recipe change.

Heirloom Tomato Soap

Not just for salads and sandwiches, tomatoes are rich in lycopene and other natural phytochemicals that are wonderful for your skin, making them a popular addition to facial soaps. The color scheme of this recipe was inspired by the beautiful natural swirls and warm tones found in the heirloom tomatoes growing in my garden, but you can leave out the natural colorants for a light orange to peach-tinted soap from just the tomatoes instead. As with some of the other recipes in this book, cocoa (or kokum) butter was added to help increase the hardness of palm-free recipes. I paired this soap with a citrusy essential oil blend, to harmonize with its bright color scheme, but you could also leave it completely unscented and suitable for more sensitive skin types.

YIELD: 7 TO 8 BARS OF SOAP (2.5 LBS/1.13 KG)

6 oz (170 g) fresh tomatoes

About 5 oz (142 g) distilled water

3.9 oz (111 g) sodium hydroxide (lye)

6.5 oz (184 g) coconut oil (23.2%)

3.5 oz (99 g) cocoa or kokum butter (12.5%)

15 oz (425 g) olive oil (53.6%)

3 oz (85 g) sweet almond or sunflower oil (10.7%)

¾ tsp red Brazilian clay mixed with 1 tbsp (15 ml) water

1 tsp (3.5 g) lemon peel powder mixed with 2 tbsp (30 ml) water

0.88 oz (25 g) orange essential oil (use a folded or Valencia type) (optional)

0.28 oz (8 g) litsea essential oil (optional)

0.14 oz (4 g) patchouli essential oil (about 1⅜ tsp) (optional)

TO MAKE THE TOMATO JUICE

Using a blender or small food processor, thoroughly blend the fresh tomatoes to a fine puree. Press the tomatoes through a sieve to remove seeds. Add enough distilled water to the resulting juice so that the total liquid weight is 9 ounces (255 g). Chill for several hours before using.

TO MAKE THE TOMATO SOAP

Wearing protective gloves and eyewear, carefully stir the lye into the chilled tomato juice. Set the lye solution aside in a safe place to cool for about 30 to 40 minutes or until the temperature drops to around 100 to 110°F (38 to 43°C). Melt the coconut oil and cocoa butter, then add to the other oils. Combine the warm oils with the cooled lye solution. Using a combination of hand stirring and an immersion blender, stir the soap until it reaches a very light trace.

At trace, stir in the essential oils, if using. Divide the soap into two equal portions of around 21 ounces (595 g) each. In one half of the soap batter, stir in the red Brazilian clay mixture. Stir the lemon peel powder mixture into the remaining half of the soap batter.

Using the In the Pot Swirl instructions on page 177, pour the two different colors of soap batter into the mold. Cover lightly with a sheet of wax or freezer paper, then a towel or light blanket. Peek at the soap every so often; if it starts developing a crack, move it to a cooler location. Keep the soap in the mold for 1 to 2 days, or until it's easy to remove, then slice it into bars when it's firm enough not to stick to your cutting tool. Cure on coated cooling racks or sheets of wax paper about 4 weeks before using.

SUBSTITUTION: To replace the cocoa or kokum butter, try using lard or tallow instead. The lye amount will stay within an acceptable range for either change and will not need to be adjusted.

Fresh Aloe & Cucumber Soap

Soothing fresh aloe and cucumbers are loaded with nutrients and beneficial compounds to revitalize and brighten your skin. The natural green hue of this soap is derived from wheatgrass powder added to the lye solution, but if you're allergic, you can substitute another green colorant option instead (see pages 145 to 154). High in skin conditioning olive and sweet almond (or sunflower) oil, this gentle soap is especially nice for those with sensitive skin. If desired, peppermint essential oil can be added for its cooling and refreshing effect, which is especially nice during hot summer weather. Alternatively, you can substitute spearmint essential oil instead, for a milder mint scent, or omit the essential oil completely, for an unscented variation.

YIELD: 7 TO 8 BARS OF SOAP (2.5 LBS/1.13 KG)

1.75 oz (50 g) chopped fresh aloe

1 oz (28 g) chopped fresh cucumber

3 oz (85 g) distilled water

Additional distilled water, as needed

3.9 oz (111 g) sodium hydroxide (lye)

2 tsp (6 g) wheatgrass powder

7 oz (198 g) coconut oil (25%)

16 oz (454 g) olive oil (57.1%)

4 oz (113 g) sweet almond or sunflower oil (14.3%)

1 oz (28 g) castor oil (3.6%)

0.88 oz (25 g) peppermint essential oil (optional)

TO MAKE THE ALOE AND CUCUMBER JUICE

Using a blender or small food processor, thoroughly blend the fresh aloe, cucumber and 3 ounces (85 g) of distilled water together. Press through a strainer to remove seeds and large pieces. Add enough distilled water to the resulting juice so that the total liquid weight is 8.75 ounces (248 g). Chill for several hours before using.

TO MAKE THE SOAP

Wearing protective gloves and eyewear, carefully stir the lye into the chilled aloe and cucumber juice. Let cool for 5 minutes, and then stir in the wheatgrass powder. Set the lye solution aside in a safe place to cool for about 30 to 40 minutes or until the temperature drops to around 100 to 110°F (38 to 43°C). Melt the coconut oil, then add to the other oils. Combine the warm oils with the cooled lye solution. Using a combination of hand stirring and an immersion blender, stir the soap until it reaches a very light trace.

At trace, stir in the essential oil, if using, then pour into a prepared mold. Cover lightly with a sheet of wax or freezer paper, then a towel or light blanket. Peek at the soap every so often; if it starts developing a crack, move it to a cooler location. Keep the soap in the mold for 1 to 2 days, or until it's easy to remove, then slice it into bars when it's firm enough not to stick to your cutting tool. Cure on coated cooling racks or sheets of wax paper about 4 or 5 weeks before using. Because of the high olive oil content, this soap will likely start off slightly softer than other soaps and may require a longer cure time to harden.

SUBSTITUTION: If castor oil is unavailable, you can use more olive oil in its place, keeping in mind that castor oil helps boost lather while olive oil does not, so your soap will be less bubbly. The lye amount will stay within an acceptable range and will not need to be adjusted.

Sunny Corn Silk & Sunflower Soap

This cheerful soap contains corn silk and sunflower petals for their skin soothing and conditioning properties. Both botanicals are steeped together into a tea and chilled before using in place of water in the lye solution. Olive and sunflower oil condition the skin, while tallow or lard supplies the hardness that would normally be provided by palm oil. (See the substitution box below for a vegan variation.) I chose to scent this soap with a sunny citrus combination, but you could alternatively leave it unscented or try another essential oil blend combination (see page 155).

YIELD: 7 TO 8 BARS OF SOAP (2.5 LBS/1.13 KG)

8.75 oz (248 g) chilled sunflower and corn silk tea (see page 165)

3.85 oz (109 g) sodium hydroxide (lye)

½ tsp annatto seed powder

6 oz (170 g) coconut oil (21.4%)

4 oz (113 g) tallow or lard (14.3%)

14 oz (397 g) olive oil (50%)

4 oz (113 g) sunflower oil (14.3%)

0.88 oz (25 g) orange essential oil (use a folded or Valencia type)

0.35 oz (10 g) grapefruit essential oil

0.18 oz (5 g) litsea or lemongrass essential oil (about 1¾ tsp)

Wearing protective gloves and eyewear, carefully stir the lye into the chilled sunflower and corn silk tea. The lye will turn a shade of yellow, but this is normal. Stir in the annatto seed powder, and then set the lye solution aside in a safe place to cool for about 30 to 40 minutes or until the temperature drops to around 100 to 110°F (38 to 43°C). To reduce the number of speckles in the finished soap, you can strain the lye mixture through a fine mesh stainless steel sieve after it cools. Melt the coconut oil and tallow, then add to the other oils. Combine the warm oils with the cooled lye solution. Using a combination of hand stirring and an immersion blender, stir the soap until it reaches a very light trace. The soap batter may look more orange than yellow, but it will lighten up over cure time.

At trace, stir in the essential oils, then pour into a prepared mold. Cover lightly with a sheet of wax or freezer paper, then a towel or light blanket. Peek at the soap every so often; if it starts developing a crack, move it to a cooler location. Keep the soap in the mold for 1 to 2 days, or until it's easy to remove, then slice it into bars when it's firm enough not to stick to your cutting tool. Cure on coated cooling racks or sheets of wax paper about 4 weeks before using. This soap starts out a bright yellow or yellow-orange color, but will fade after several months.

SUBSTITUTION: To replace the tallow or lard, try using cocoa or kokum butter instead. The lye amount will stay within an acceptable range for either change and will not need to be adjusted.

Soaps from the Farm

Goat and cow's milk contain a range of vitamins and nutrients, including lactic acid, an alpha hydroxy acid that's used to improve the appearance of skin. These milks also add an extra creamy and luxurious feel to the finished soap.

While these recipes were specifically designed for use with animal milks, if you're allergic or want to keep your soap vegan, you can substitute with plant-based milks instead. Thanks to its lauric acid content, coconut milk will help your soap have a bubblier lather. Almond milk is high in essential fatty acids and will give your finished soap a creamy, nourishing lather. Oat milk contains naturally soothing compounds that are great for sensitive or irritated skin.

Since milk is a somewhat delicate ingredient that can easily overheat during the soapmaking process, it requires a bit of extra care in handling. If you're new to using milk in soaps, be sure to read the section on adding milk to soap on page 166 before making your first one.

Less commonly used in soapmaking recipes, egg yolks add protein and other nutrients to your creations. They're especially popular in shampoo bars because of their reputation for encouraging thick healthy hair growth. For a fun recipe to try using yolks, check out Vanilla Bean & Egg Yolk Soap on page 83.

A lovely way to enrich milk soaps is to first infuse the milk with flowers specifically known for their anti-inflammatory and skin-soothing properties such as chamomile, calendula, dandelion and lavender. See Cottage Garden Soaps (page 86) for an example of this method.

Goat Milk Shampoo Bars

This shampoo bar has a generous helping of castor oil to promote a great lathering experience, along with a full amount of goat's milk for an added creamy and luxurious feel. Shea or mango butter helps to slightly harden the finished bars while providing moisturizing properties for scalp and hair. I chose to scent these bars with a floral blend of essential oils, but see the blend ideas on page 155 for alternate ideas. If you've never made milk soap before, be sure to read the detailed instructional section about adding milk to soap on page 166 before making this recipe.

YIELD: 7 TO 8 BARS OF SOAP (2.5 LBS/1.13 KG)

8.5 oz (241 g) frozen goat's milk

0.5 oz (14 g) distilled water

3.9 oz (111 g) sodium hydroxide (lye)

7.5 oz (213 g) coconut oil (26.8%)

3 oz (85 g) shea or mango butter (10.7%)

10.5 oz (298 g) olive oil (37.5%)

3 oz (85 g) sweet almond or sunflower oil (10.7%)

4 oz (113 g) castor oil (14.3%)

0.85 oz (24 g) lavender essential oil (optional)

0.21 oz (6 g) litsea essential oil (about 2 tsp) (optional)

0.14 oz (4 g) clary sage essential oil (about 1¼ tsp) (optional)

Place the frozen goat's milk and water in a heavy-duty plastic or stainless steel bowl. Wearing protective gloves and eyewear, carefully sprinkle a small amount of lye at a time over the frozen milk, stirring well after each addition. The entire process will take several minutes, but working slowly ensures that the milk doesn't scorch and that the lye completely dissolves. The lye solution does not need to cool further before the addition of the oils. Melt the coconut oil and shea butter, then add to the other oils. Add the lye and milk solution to the oils. Using a combination of hand stirring and an immersion blender, stir the soap until it reaches a very light trace.

At trace, stir in essential oils, if using, then pour into a prepared mold. If you'd like to prevent gel phase (see page 21), place the filled mold in your refrigerator for 24 hours. If you'd like the soap to go through gel phase, as I did here, cover the mold lightly with a sheet of wax or freezer paper, then a light dish towel or pillowcase. Peek at the soap every so often; if it starts developing a crack, move it to a cooler location. Soap that's kept cool and doesn't go through gel phase will be lighter in color than soaps that do go through gel phase. Keep the soap in the mold for 1 to 2 days, or until it's easy to remove, then slice it into bars when it's firm enough not to stick to your cutting tool. Cure on coated cooling racks or sheets of wax paper about 4 weeks before using.

SUBSTITUTION: If allergic to coconut oil, try using an equal amount of babassu oil in its place. The lye amount should be slightly reduced, to 3.85 ounces (109 g).

To replace the shea or mango butter, try using lard or tallow instead. The lye amount will stay within an acceptable range for either change and will not need to be adjusted.

Lavender Milk Bath Bars

Powdered milk is a popular addition to bath soaks for its creamy moisturizing properties, but can easily be included in bar soaps for similar benefits as well. This milk bath bar carries the delightful scent of lavender for its ability to calm and relax harried minds, while its lovely natural hue is provided by purple Brazilian clay. Since milk powder can often turn your soap shades of tan or light brown, I added white kaolin clay to the lye solution to help brighten and whiten the basic soap color, allowing the purple clay's color to shine through more clearly.

YIELD: 7 TO 8 BARS OF SOAP (2.5 LBS/1.13 KG)

9 oz (255 g) distilled water

3.95 oz (112 g) sodium hydroxide (lye)

2 tsp (7.7 g) purple Brazilian clay

2 tsp (5 g) white kaolin clay

7 oz (198 g) coconut oil (25%)

5 oz (142 g) tallow or lard (17.85%)

12 oz (340 g) olive oil (42.85%)

4 oz (113 g) sweet almond or sunflower oil (14.3%)

2 tsp (5 g) dry powdered milk (cow, goat or coconut)

1.23 oz (35 g) lavender essential oil

Wearing protective gloves and eyewear, carefully stir the lye into the distilled water. Stir in the purple and white clays until completely dissolved, then set the lye solution aside in a safe place to cool for about 30 to 40 minutes or until the temperature drops to around 100 to 110°F (38 to 43°C). Melt the coconut oil and tallow, then add to the other oils. Add the powdered milk to the warm oils and blend thoroughly with an immersion blender until no lumps remain. Add the cooled lye solution to the warm oils and powdered milk mixture. Using a combination of hand stirring and an immersion blender, stir the soap until it reaches a very light trace.

At trace, stir in the lavender essential oil then pour into a prepared mold. If you'd like to prevent gel phase (see page 21), place the filled mold in your refrigerator for 24 hours. If you'd like it to go through gel phase, as I did with the soap shown, cover the mold lightly with a sheet of wax or freezer paper, then a light dish towel or pillowcase. Peek at the soap every so often; if it starts developing a crack, move it to a cooler location. Keep the soap in the mold for 1 to 2 days, or until it's easy to remove, then slice it into bars when it's firm enough not to stick to your cutting tool. Cure on coated cooling racks or sheets of wax paper about 4 weeks before using.

SUBSTITUTION: Replace the tallow or lard with 4 ounces (113 g) of kokum or cocoa butter plus 1 ounce (28 g) of castor oil. The lye amount will change slightly to 3.9 ounces (111 g).

Classic Oatmeal, Milk & Honey Soap

This popular soap combination is well loved by many, for good reason. The proteins and natural sugars in fresh milk act as a skin conditioner and lather booster, while oats soothe dry itchy skin. Honey is a natural nourishing humectant that helps skin retain a healthy glow. I left this classic unscented, so that the finished soap carries just the faintest whiff of natural oats and honey, but feel free to add an essential oil, such as lavender, if you'd like. (See page 155 for more on adding essential oils to soap.)

YIELD: 7 TO 8 BARS OF SOAP (2.5 LBS/1.13 KG)

8.5 oz (241 g) frozen milk

0.5 oz (14 g) distilled water

3.95 oz (112 g) sodium hydroxide (lye)

7 oz (198 g) coconut oil (25%)

7 oz (198 g) lard or tallow (25%)

14 oz (397 g) olive oil (50%)

1 tsp (5 ml) honey mixed with 1 tsp (5 ml) water

1 tbsp (7 g) powdered oats

1.06 to 1.23 oz (30 to 35 g) essential oil of your choice (optional)

Place the frozen milk and water in a heavy-duty plastic or stainless steel bowl. Wearing protective gloves and eyewear, carefully sprinkle a small amount of lye at a time over the frozen milk, stirring well after each addition. The entire process will take several minutes, but working slowly ensures that the milk doesn't scorch and that the lye completely dissolves. The lye solution does not need to cool before the addition of the oils. Melt the coconut oil and lard or tallow, then add to the olive oil. Add the lye and milk solution to the oils. Using a combination of hand stirring and an immersion blender, stir the soap until it reaches a very light trace.

At trace, stir in the honey and water mixture, powdered oats and essential oil, if using, then pour into a prepared mold. If you'd like to prevent gel phase (see page 21), place the filled mold in your refrigerator for 24 hours. If you'd like the soap to go through gel phase, as I did here, cover the mold lightly with a sheet of wax or freezer paper, then a light dish towel or pillowcase. Peek at the soap every so often; if it starts developing a crack, move it to a cooler location. Soap that's kept cool and doesn't go through gel phase will be lighter in color than soaps that do go through gel phase. Keep the soap in the mold for 1 to 2 days, or until it's easy to remove, then slice it into bars when it's firm enough not to stick to your cutting tool. Cure on coated cooling racks or sheets of wax paper about 4 weeks before using.

SUBSTITUTION: Replace the 7 ounces (198 g) of tallow or lard with a combination of 3.5 ounces (99 g) kokum or cocoa butter plus 1.5 ounces (43 g) castor oil plus 2 ounces (57 g) sunflower or sweet almond oil. The lye amount will change slightly to 3.9 ounces (111 g).

Vanilla Bean & Egg Yolk Soap

Lecithin-rich egg yolk adds protein and vitamins to this creamy soap while specks of vanilla bean offer a touch of exfoliation and visual interest. I used unrefined cocoa butter in this recipe since I wanted its natural scent to remain in the finished bars. Skin nourishing sweet almond oil or sunflower oil moisturizes and soothes skin, while coconut oil provides lather. The naturally high pH of soap helps preserve and prevent spoilage, even with the fresh egg included. I don't recommend hot processing this recipe as it needs to stay cool to prevent the egg from overheating.

YIELD: 7 TO 8 BARS OF SOAP (2.5 LBS/1.13 KG)

8.5 oz (241 g) distilled water

3.9 oz (111 g) sodium hydroxide (lye)

7 oz (198 g) coconut oil (25%)

4 oz (113 g) unrefined cocoa butter (14.3%)

14 oz (397 g) olive oil (50%)

3 oz (85 g) sweet almond or sunflower oil (10.7%)

1 vanilla bean

1 room temperature egg yolk, beaten

Wearing protective gloves and eyewear, carefully stir the lye into the distilled water. Set the lye solution aside in a safe place to cool for about 30 to 40 minutes or until the temperature drops to around 100 to 110°F (38 to 43°C). Melt the coconut oil and cocoa butter, then add to the other oils. Split the vanilla bean, scrape the inside into the warm oils and mix so the vanilla specks are evenly distributed. Temper the egg yolk by removing about a cup (240 ml) of the warm oil and vanilla bean mixture and stir together with the beaten egg yolk. Return the yolk/oil mixture to the remaining oils and blend until thoroughly incorporated. Add the cooled lye solution. Using a combination of hand stirring and an immersion blender, stir the soap until it reaches a very light trace.

At trace, pour into a prepared mold. This soap does best when kept on the cooler side, so you may want to consider individual molds to prevent partial gel phase (see page 21 for more on gel phase) and/or tucking the soap in the refrigerator for 12 to 24 hours after pouring.

Keep the soap in the mold for 1 to 2 days, or until it's easy to remove, then slice it into bars or unmold individual bars. Cure on coated cooling racks or sheets of wax paper about 4 weeks before using.

TIP: While you may be tempted to try adding commonly found vanilla baking extract to your recipes, the scent won't survive the soapmaking process, plus the alcohol content can make your soap seize. Vanilla absolute and vanilla oleoresin are two options that can add a subtle hint of vanilla scent to soap, but they can be difficult to source and are cost-prohibitive, so I did not include them in this recipe.

SUBSTITUTION: To replace the cocoa butter, try using kokum butter, lard or tallow instead. The lye amount will stay within an acceptable range for all options and will not need to be adjusted.

Milk Chocolate Mint Soap

The delicious natural chocolate scent of unrefined cocoa butter combines with peppermint essential oil to create this soap that smells just like your favorite peppermint chocolate candy! Cocoa powder colors half of the soap light brown, while French green clay tints the other half minty green. Since milk can turn your soap various shades of tan, leading to muddied natural colorants, white kaolin clay is added to the lye mixture to lighten the soap base to ensure that the green clay's color shines through.

YIELD: 7 TO 8 BARS OF SOAP (2.5 LBS/1.13 KG)

8.5 oz (241 g) frozen milk

0.5 oz (14 g) distilled water

3.9 oz (111 g) sodium hydroxide (lye)

2 tsp (5 g) white kaolin clay

6.5 oz (184 g) coconut oil (23.2%)

4 oz (113 g) unrefined cocoa butter (14.3%)

14 oz (397 g) olive oil (50%)

3.5 oz (99 g) rice bran oil (12.5)

1 tsp (2 g) cocoa powder

1.06 oz (30 g) peppermint essential oil

2 tsp (9.5 g) French green clay mixed with 2 tbsp (30 ml) water

Place the frozen milk and water in a heavy-duty plastic or stainless steel bowl. Wearing protective gloves and eyewear, carefully sprinkle a small amount of lye at a time over the frozen milk, stirring well after each addition. The entire process will take several minutes, but working slowly ensures that the milk doesn't scorch and that the lye completely dissolves. Stir the white kaolin clay into the lye and milk solution. The lye solution does not need to cool before the addition of the oils. Melt the coconut oil and cocoa butter, then add to the other oils. Remove 1 tablespoon (15 ml) from the combined warm oils and stir together with the cocoa powder in a separate small bowl. Set aside until needed. Add the lye and milk solution to the oils. Using a combination of hand stirring and an immersion blender, stir the soap until it reaches a very light trace.

Divide the soap batter equally into two containers. In one container of soap batter, stir in the cocoa powder and oil mixture until well blended. In the second container of soap batter, thoroughly stir in the French green clay and water mixture. You may need to briefly use an immersion blender in each container, to ensure even mixing.

Following the directions on page 170, pour the chocolate soap batter into the bottom of a prepared mold. If you'd like to make a pencil line between the layers, lightly sprinkle cocoa powder over the first layer. (See page 173 for more on making pencil lines in soap.) Next, pour the green layer of soap. If desired, texturize the top of the soap. (See page 168 for tips on adding texture to soap tops.)

Tuck the soap in your refrigerator for about 24 hours, then remove to room temperature. The soap will still be soft, so keep it in the mold an additional day or two until it's easy to remove. Slice it into bars when it's firm enough not to stick to your cutting tool and cure on coated cooling racks or sheets of wax paper about 4 weeks before using.

SUBSTITUTION: The rice bran oil can be replaced with sweet almond or sunflower oil, with no need to change the amount of lye in the recipe.

Cottage Garden Soaps

In this recipe, milk is used instead of water to make a floral infusion for the lye solution. In the variations section, I give several flower and essential oil combinations that I enjoy making, but you can use other herbs or flowers that you like best. Something to keep in mind when experimenting is that strong darkly colored infusions can discolor soap to shades of brown or orange-brown (herbs like mint and basil leaves tend to do this). When topping soap, always use completely dried flowers to prevent mold from developing and gently press them into the soap batter while wearing gloves. When you're ready to slice the bars, turn them on their sides so you don't leave drag marks from the herbs over the soap. (See page 168 for more on topping soaps.)

YIELD: 7 TO 8 BARS OF SOAP (2.5 LBS/1.13 KG)

8.5 oz (241 g) flower-infused frozen milk (see page 166 for how to infuse milk)

0.5 oz (14 g) distilled water

3.9 oz (111 g) sodium hydroxide (lye)

6 oz (170 g) coconut oil (21.4%)

7 oz (198 g) lard or tallow (25%)

15 oz (425 g) olive oil (53.6%)

1.06 to 1.41 oz (30 to 40 g) essential oils (see opposite page for suggested blends)

Dried flowers, for topping

Place the flower-infused frozen milk and water in a heavy-duty plastic or stainless steel bowl. Wearing protective gloves and eyewear, carefully sprinkle a small amount of lye at a time over the frozen milk, stirring well after each addition. The entire process will take several minutes, but working slowly ensures that the milk doesn't scorch and that the lye completely dissolves. The lye solution does not need to be cooled before adding the oils. Melt the coconut oil and lard or tallow, then add to the olive oil. Add the lye and milk solution to the oils. Using a combination of hand stirring and an immersion blender, stir the soap until it reaches a very light trace.

At trace, stir in the essential oils, if using, then pour into a prepared mold. Decorate with dried flowers, if desired. If you'd like to prevent gel phase (see page 21), place the filled mold in your refrigerator for 24 hours. If you'd like the soap to go through gel phase, cover the mold lightly with a sheet of wax or freezer paper, then a light dish towel or pillowcase. Soap that goes through gel phase will turn a darker shade of tan or brown than soap that doesn't go through gel phase. Peek at the soap every so often; if it starts developing a crack, move it to a cooler location. Keep the soap in the mold for 1 to 2 days, or until it's easy to remove, then slice it into bars when it's firm enough not to stick to your cutting tool. Cure on coated cooling racks or sheets of wax paper about 4 weeks before using.

*See photo on page 74.

SUBSTITUTION: For a vegan option, use unsweetened, unflavored non-dairy milk and replace the 7 ounces (198 g) of tallow or lard with a combination of 3.5 ounces (99 g) kokum or cocoa butter plus 1.5 ounces (43 g) castor oil plus 2 ounces (57 g) sunflower or sweet almond oil. The lye amount will change slightly to 3.85 ounces (109 g).

Suggested flower and essential oil combinations:

FOR LAVENDER-INFUSED MILK SOAP
Milk infused with ½ cup (12 g) lavender flowers
1.23 oz (35 g) lavender essential oil
Dried lavender buds, for topping

FOR ROSE-INFUSED SOAP
Milk infused with ½ cup (4 g) rose petals
1.06 oz (30 g) geranium essential oil
Dried rose petals or rosebuds, for topping

FOR CALENDULA-INFUSED SOAP
Milk infused with ½ cup (4 g) calendula flowers
0.88 oz (25 g) orange (folded type or Valencia), 0.35 oz (10 g) litsea and 0.18 oz (5 g) lemongrass essential oils
Dried calendula flowers and cornflower (bachelor button) petals, for topping

FOR CHAMOMILE & DANDELION-INFUSED SOAP
Milk infused with ¼ cup each of chamomile (5 g) and dandelion (2 g) flowers
0.88 oz (25 g) litsea, 0.35 oz (10 g) grapefruit and 0.18 oz (5 g) clary sage essential oils
Dried helichrysum flowers, blue cornflower (bachelor button) petals and rose petals, for topping

Soaps from the Sea

Inspired by breezy sunny days on the beach, these recipes incorporate popular ingredients such as sea salt, coconut milk and sea clay.

Seaweed, another interesting addition to soap, as shown in Sea Salt & Seaweed Soap on page 101, has been studied for its ability to revitalize skin and the potential to treat tough conditions such as psoriasis. High in nutrients that promote healthy shiny hair, seaweed is a stellar ingredient for shampoo bars too.

Salt and brine bars, such as Cambrian Blue Cooling Salt Bars, page 93, and Citrus Breeze Brine Bars on page 90, are a fun break from your standard soap recipes. They go to show that some soapmaking rules can be broken with their higher than normal amounts of coconut oil and generous helpings of sea salt. If you like rock hard soaps with a terrific lather, you'll certainly want to give salt and brine bars a try!

If you're up for a challenge, try your hand at creating a batch of Beach Bum Layered Soap, found on page 97. It contains several natural colorants and consists of three layers, reminiscent of a seascape.

Citrus Breeze Brine Bars

In brine bar recipes, a significant amount of salt is added to the lye solution, creating a brine that provides extra hardness and a smooth finish to the final bars. While this results in a more solid bar of soap, the extra salt will diminish lather. To offset that characteristic, brine bars have a higher than normal amount of coconut oil, which lathers well in salt water, plus added castor oil to help boost bubbles. A higher superfat of around 10 percent (see page 18 for more on superfat) is calculated into the recipe to prevent the extra coconut oil from being too drying for some skin types. Coconut water can be used in this recipe to slightly increase lather and add label appeal, but if none is available, plain distilled water works well too. Brine soaps are often difficult to slice into bars without them crumbling, so individual molds are recommended for best results.

YIELD: 7 TO 8 BARS OF SOAP (2.5 LBS/1.13 KG)

9.5 oz (269 g) coconut water or distilled water

3.95 oz (112 g) sodium hydroxide (lye)

1.5 oz (43 g) sea salt

12 oz (340 g) coconut oil (42.9%)

10 oz (283 g) olive oil (35.7%)

4 oz (113 g) sunflower oil (14.3%)

2 oz (57 g) castor oil (7.1%)

0.88 oz (25 g) 10× (ten-fold) orange essential oil

0.53 oz (15 g) grapefruit essential oil

Wearing protective gloves and eyewear, carefully stir the lye into the distilled water until completely dissolved. Next, stir in the salt until completely dissolved. Set aside to cool for about 30 to 40 minutes or until the temperature drops to around 100 to 110°F (38 to 43°C). Melt the coconut oil, then add to the other oils. Combine the warm oils with the cooled lye solution. Using a combination of hand stirring and an immersion blender, stir the soap until it reaches a very light trace.

At trace, stir in the essential oils, then pour into individual molds. Cover lightly with a sheet of wax or freezer paper, then a towel or light blanket. Peek at the soap every so often; if it starts developing a crack, move it to a cooler location. Keep the soap in the molds for 1 day, or until easy to remove and when firm enough not to stick to your cutting tool. Cure on coated cooling racks or sheets of wax paper about 4 weeks before using.

SUBSTITUTION: If castor oil is unavailable, you can use more olive oil in its place, keeping in mind that castor oil helps boost lather while olive oil does not, so your soap will be less bubbly. The lye amount will stay within an acceptable range and will not need to be adjusted.

Cambrian Blue Cooling Salt Bars

As refreshing as a splash in the ocean, these pretty sea salt bars are naturally colored with Cambrian blue clay, an incredibly mineral-rich treasure mined from the salt lakes of Siberia. Like brine bars (see recipe on page 90), in that they contain added salt to increase bar hardness, salt bars differ in that you stir in the salt at trace instead of dissolving it in the lye solution. This allows you to add much more salt to the recipe, up to an equal amount as the weight of the oils, creating rock-hard bars of soap that have a coarser, more exfoliating texture than brine bars. Salt bars are most often made with 80 to 100 percent coconut oil, since that's one oil that still lathers in the presence of salt. The superfat (see page 18) of 20 percent is higher than normal in this recipe to offset coconut oil's high cleansing properties. Sunflower oil was added to help nourish and protect skin, but sweet almond oil will perform just as beautifully. Salt bars harden up in a matter of hours, so it can be difficult to slice into bars without them crumbling. For this reason, individual molds are recommended for best results.

YIELD: 7 TO 8 BARS OF SOAP (2.5 LBS/1.13 KG)

9 oz (255 g) distilled water

3.95 oz (112 g) sodium hydroxide (lye)

3 tbsp (30 g) Cambrian blue clay

24 oz (680 g) coconut oil (85.7%)

4 oz (113 g) sunflower or sweet almond oil (14.3%)

1.06 oz (30 g) peppermint essential oil

26 oz (737 g) sea salt

Wearing protective gloves and eyewear, carefully stir the lye into the distilled water. Stir in the blue clay. Set the lye solution aside to cool for about 30 to 40 minutes or until the temperature drops to around 100 to 110°F (38 to 43°C). Melt the coconut oil and add to the sunflower oil. Combine the warm oils with the cooled lye solution. Using a combination of hand stirring and an immersion blender, stir the soap until it reaches a light trace.

At trace, stir in the essential oil. Next, hand-stir in the sea salt. At this point, the batter will start getting very thick. Working quickly, pour the soap batter into individual molds. Cover lightly with a sheet of wax or freezer paper, then a towel or light blanket. Peek at the soap every so often; if it starts developing a crack, move it to a cooler location. The soap will probably be firm enough to unmold in 2 to 3 hours, but it still needs to be handled with gloves for the first 24 hours. Cure on coated cooling racks or sheets of wax paper about 4 weeks before using.

> TIP: If Cambrian clay isn't available, you can use any other type of clay in its place or see pages 145 to 154 for more natural colorant options.

Rejuvenating Dead Sea Clay Facial Bars

Rich in minerals and nutrients, Dead Sea clay gently cleanses and tones dull flaky skin. Unrefined hemp seed oil subtly enhances the soap's natural green hue while providing essential fatty acids. Lecithin-rich sunflower oil protects and soothes damaged skin, but sweet almond oil can be used instead for a similar effect. For a fresh clean scent, I chose a combination of calming lavender and camphorous tea tree essential oils, but you may wish to use an alternative blend (see pages 155 to 160) or leave the soap unscented altogether.

YIELD: 7 TO 8 BARS OF SOAP (2.5 LBS/1.13 KG)

8.5 oz (241 g) distilled water

3.95 oz (112 g) sodium hydroxide (lye)

1½ tbsp (7 g) Dead Sea clay powder

8 oz (227 g) coconut oil (28.6%)

2.5 oz (71 g) unrefined hemp oil (8.9%)

14.5 oz (411 g) olive oil (51.8%)

3 oz (85 g) sunflower or sweet almond oil (10.7%)

0.85 oz (24 g) lavender essential oil

0.28 oz (8 g) tea tree essential oil

Wearing protective gloves and eyewear, carefully stir the lye into the distilled water. Stir in the Dead Sea clay powder, then set the lye solution aside in a safe place to cool for about 30 to 40 minutes or until the temperature drops to around 100 to 110°F (38 to 43°C). Melt the coconut oil, then add to the other oils. Combine the warm oils with the cooled lye solution. Using a combination of hand stirring and an immersion blender, stir the soap until it reaches a light trace.

At trace, stir in the essential oils, then pour into a prepared mold. Cover lightly with a sheet of wax or freezer paper, then a towel or light blanket. Peek at the soap every so often; if it starts developing a crack, move it to a cooler location. Keep the soap in the mold for 1 to 2 days, or until it's easy to remove, then slice it into bars when it's firm enough not to stick to your cutting tool. Cure on coated cooling racks or sheets of wax paper about 4 weeks before using.

SUBSTITUTION: If hemp oil isn't available, try using avocado or kukui nut oil instead, without needing to change lye amount.

Coconut oil can be replaced in equal measure with babassu oil. The lye amount will decrease slightly to 3.9 ounces (111 g).

Beach Bum Layered Soap

The triple-layered technique and lengthier ingredient list make this soap recipe best suited for the adventurous soapmaker who has several successful batches under their belt. Coconut milk and oil enhance the creamy lather of this soap while kokum butter adds some of the hardness that palm oil usually provides. Patchouli, lavender and cedarwood essential oils combine to create a delightfully happy hippy scent, but you can substitute with other essential oils (see pages 155 to 160) if you wish. A layer including real sand adds a bit of exfoliation, but if you don't have clean beach sand available, it can be left out.

YIELD: 7 TO 8 BARS OF SOAP (2.5 LBS/1.13 KG)

5.75 oz (163 g) distilled water

3.9 oz (111 g) sodium hydroxide (lye)

3 oz (85 g) coconut milk

7.5 oz (213 g) coconut oil (26.8%)

3.5 oz (99 g) kokum or cocoa butter (12.5%)

14 oz (397 g) olive oil (50%)

3 oz (85 g) sunflower or sweet almond oil (10.7%)

0.56 oz (16 g) dark patchouli essential oil

0.32 oz (9 g) lavender essential oil

0.28 oz (8 g) cedarwood Atlas essential oil

¼ tsp sand

¼ tsp lemon peel powder

5 tsp (25 g) Cambrian blue clay mixed with 3 tbsp (45 ml) distilled water

¼ tsp indigo powder mixed with 1 tbsp (15 ml) hot water

4 tsp (10 g) white kaolin clay mixed with 2 tbsp (30 ml) distilled water

Wearing protective gloves and eyewear, carefully stir the lye into the distilled water, then set the lye solution aside in a safe place to cool for about 30 to 40 minutes or until the temperature drops to around 100 to 110°F (38 to 43°C). Melt the coconut oil and kokum (or cocoa) butter, then add to the other oils. Using an immersion blender, thoroughly mix the coconut milk into the warm oils. Combine the oils and coconut milk mixture with the cooled lye solution. Using a combination of hand stirring and an immersion blender, stir the soap until it reaches a light trace. At trace, stir in the essential oils.

Weigh out 14 ounces (397 g) of soap batter into a separate container. Stir in the sand and lemon peel. Stir well until the batter is thickened. Pour the layer on the bottom of a prepared loaf mold, using a spoon or spatula to texturize the layer of sand a bit.

Stir the diluted Cambrian blue clay into the remaining soap batter then divide that in equal halves. In one half of the blue batter, add the diluted indigo mixture to form a darker blue color. Stir well until thickened, then spoon that darker blue layer into the loaf mold, using a spoon to texturize the ocean waves. In the remaining half of the blue batter, add the diluted kaolin clay to lighten the blue clay's color. Spoon into the mold, forming a light blue sky.

Cover the mold lightly with a sheet of wax or freezer paper, then a towel or light blanket. Peek at the soap every so often; if it starts developing a crack, move it to a cooler location. Keep the soap in the mold for 1 to 2 days, or until it's easy to remove, then slice it into bars. Cure on coated cooling racks or sheets of wax paper for at least 4 weeks before using.

SUBSTITUTION: To replace the kokum or cocoa butter, try using lard or tallow instead. The lye amount will stay within an acceptable range for either change and will not need to be adjusted.

Coconut Milk Shampoo Sticks

Shampoo sticks are a fun alternative to the traditional bar-shaped soap. Their smaller size makes them easy to handle and convenient to use. In this recipe, a double strength lye solution is made first, using only half the amount of water that a regular soap recipe would normally use, then coconut milk is added to the oils to make up the remaining liquid balance. With its high lauric acid content, coconut milk will ensure your soap has a bubbly lather and extra creamy feel, while jojoba oil adds a touch of luxury that's fantastic for promoting healthy shiny hair.

YIELD: 7 TO 8 BARS OF SOAP (2.5 LBS/1.13 KG)

4.5 oz (128 g) distilled water

3.85 oz (109 g) sodium hydroxide (lye)

4 oz (113 g) coconut milk

7.5 oz (213 g) coconut oil (26.8%)

12 oz (340 g) olive oil (42.9%)

3.5 oz (99 g) sunflower or sweet almond oil (12.5%)

4 oz (113 g) castor oil (14.3%)

1 oz (28 g) jojoba oil (3.5%)

Wearing protective gloves and eyewear, carefully stir the lye into the distilled water, then set the lye solution aside in a safe place to cool for about 30 to 40 minutes or until the temperature drops to around 100 to 110°F (38 to 43°C). Melt the coconut oil, then add to the other oils. Add the coconut milk to the warm oils and use an immersion blender for a few seconds until thoroughly combined. Add the lye solution to the warm oils and coconut milk mixture. Using a combination of hand stirring and an immersion blender, stir the soap until it reaches a light trace.

Pour into a prepared mold. Cover lightly with a sheet of wax or freezer paper, then a towel or light blanket. Peek at the soap every so often; if it starts developing a crack, uncover and move it to a cooler location. Keep the soap in the mold for 1 to 2 days, or until it's easy to remove, then slice it into bars when it's firm enough not to stick to your cutting tool. To make shampoo sticks, cut each bar into thirds. Cure on coated cooling racks or sheets of wax paper about 4 weeks before using.

SUBSTITUTION: If jojoba isn't available, try substituting with more sunflower or sweet almond oil in its place. The lye amount will not need to be adjusted.

Sea Salt & Seaweed Soap

Many types of seaweed, including kelp (*Laminaria* spp.), sea lettuce (*Ulva lactuca*) and Irish moss (*Chondrus crispus*), are featured in high-end cosmetics for their anti-aging, moisturizing and skin brightening benefits. Seaweeds can also be added to soap in their dried powdered form. Since they tend to have a strong fishy scent when used in excess, it's best to keep amounts on the low side and to partner them with pleasing essential oil blends. In this soap, I colored the entire batter a shade of green-blue by adding indigo powder to the lye solution and including dark green unrefined hemp oil in the recipe. I then divided the soap and stirred seaweed and French green clay into half and used the funnel pour technique (page 178) for a subtle visual contrast.

YIELD: 7 TO 8 BARS OF SOAP (2.5 LBS/1.13 KG)

8.5 oz (241 g) distilled water

3.95 oz (112 g) sodium hydroxide (lye)

2 tsp (12 g) sea salt

³/₄ tsp indigo powder

7.5 oz (213 g) coconut oil (26.8%)

14 oz (397 g) olive oil (50%)

3.5 oz (99 g) sweet almond or sunflower oil (12.5%)

3 oz (85 g) unrefined hemp or avocado oil (10.7%)

0.53 oz (15 g) peppermint essential oil

0.53 oz (15 g) lavender essential oil

1 tsp (4 g) powdered seaweed

1 tsp (4 g) French green clay mixed with 1 tbsp (15 ml) water

Wearing protective gloves and eyewear, carefully stir the lye into the distilled water. Stir in the sea salt and indigo powder. Set the lye solution aside in a safe place to cool for about 30 to 40 minutes or until the temperature drops to around 100 to 110°F (38 to 43°C). Melt the coconut oil, then add to the other oils. Combine the warm oils with the cooled lye solution. Using a combination of hand stirring and an immersion blender, stir the soap until it reaches a very light trace.

At trace, hand stir in the essential oils. Divide the soap into two equal portions. Leave half of the soap batter plain. In the other half of the soap batter, stir in the powdered seaweed and diluted French green clay.

Using the directions on page 178, alternate pouring the two colors of soap batter through a funnel to create the design shown. You may not see a noticeable contrast between the colors until the soap goes through gel phase and starts curing. Cover the soap mold lightly with a sheet of wax or freezer paper, then a towel or light blanket. Peek at the soap every so often; if it starts developing a crack, move it to a cooler location. Keep the soap in the mold for 1 to 2 days, or until it's easy to remove, then slice it into bars when it's firm enough not to stick to your cutting tool. Cure on coated cooling racks or sheets of wax paper about 4 weeks before using.

TIP: If your seaweed comes in large dried pieces or you dry your own freshly gathered pieces, run them through a coffee grinder or use a mortar and pestle until finely powdered.

SUBSTITUTION: If you're allergic to coconut oil, try using babassu oil in its place. The lye amount will decrease slightly to 3.9 ounces (111 g).

Soaps from the Apiary

Products harvested from beehives are loaded with health benefits and make fantastic additions to your handmade soaps.

Honey is a humectant, which means it attracts and retains moisture. It has an antibacterial effect and helps soften rough, aged or damaged skin. As a bonus, when honey is added to soap, the natural sugars in it help to promote a better lather, as it does in Orange Honey Shampoo Bars on page 110.

An amazing super food, bee pollen is packed with amino acids, vitamins, minerals, trace elements, protein and enzymes. It's incorporated into soaps, such as Bee Pollen & Honey Soap on page 113, and skin care products for its anti-inflammatory properties and to soften and smooth skin.

Propolis is created by bees from tree resin to seal cracks and gaps in their hive and to use as a disinfecting agent. It has remarkable antioxidant and antimicrobial levels. While its properties are best extracted by alcohol, it's easiest to incorporate propolis in soap as an oil or water infusion, as I did in Propolis & Dandelion Soap on page 106, since alcohol can cause soap to seize or generally misbehave.

Finally, beeswax is another gem from the hive. When added in small amounts, between 0.5 to 3 percent, in soap recipes, as I did in Honey & Beeswax Soap on page 109, it hardens soap and reduces the risk of soda ash (see page 184) from developing.

Sweet Honey & Shea Layers Soap

This recipe uses honey's natural tendency to darken soap to create a simple contrasting layered design. A generous amount of shea or mango butter and sweet almond or sunflower oil moisturizes and nourishes skin while castor oil ensures an abundant lather. The layers of soap are separated with a thin pencil line made of cocoa powder to provide visual contrast.

YIELD: 7 TO 8 BARS OF SOAP (2.5 LBS/1.13 KG)

9 oz (255 g) distilled water

3.85 oz (109 g) sodium hydroxide (lye)

7 oz (198 g) coconut oil (25%)

4 oz (113 g) shea or mango butter (14.3%)

11 oz (312 g) olive oil (39.3%)

3 oz (85 g) sweet almond or sunflower oil (10.7%)

3 oz (85 g) castor oil (10.7%)

1½ tsp (7.5 ml) honey mixed with 1½ tsp (7.5 ml) warm water

Cocoa powder, for creating a pencil line, if desired

Wearing protective gloves and eyewear, carefully stir the lye into the distilled water, then set the lye solution aside in a safe place to cool for about 30 to 40 minutes or until the temperature drops to around 100 to 110°F (38 to 43°C). Melt the coconut oil and shea butter, then add to the other oils. Combine the warm oils with the cooled lye solution. Using a combination of hand stirring and an immersion blender, stir the soap until it reaches a light trace.

At trace, divide the batter evenly in half between two containers. Leave one container of soap batter plain. Stir the diluted honey into the second container of soap. Pour the plain layer of soap in the bottom of a prepared mold. If you'd like to make a pencil line between the layers, lightly sprinkle cocoa powder over the first layer. (See page 173 for more on making pencil lines in soap.) Carefully pour the remaining soap batter into the mold, forming the second layer. At first, both the plain soap and the honey-enriched soap will look the same shade, but as it warms up in the mold, the color of the honey portion will become more visible. Cover lightly with a sheet of wax or freezer paper, then a towel or light blanket. Peek at the soap every so often; if it starts developing a crack, move it to a cooler location. Keep the soap in the mold for 1 to 2 days, or until it's easy to remove, then slice it into bars when it's firm enough not to stick to your cutting tool. Cure on coated cooling racks or sheets of wax paper about 4 weeks before using.

SUBSTITUTION: To replace the shea or mango butter, try using lard or tallow instead. The lye amount will stay within an acceptable range for either change and will not need to be adjusted.

Propolis & Dandelion Soap

Propolis is a substance bees create from tree resins and use as a disinfectant and to seal gaps in their hives. It's rich in antioxidants and antimicrobial properties. The most potent propolis extracts are alcohol-based, however, those aren't practical for soapmaking because the alcohol content can cause problems in soap. Fortunately, some of the beneficial properties of propolis can be transferred into water and oil infusions, which can both be incorporated into your favorite soap recipes. I chose to include dandelion-infused olive oil in this recipe, but feel free to use another herbal infusion instead, such as chamomile or calendula. When picking dandelion flowers in the spring, remember that they're an early food source for pollinators, so leave plenty of flowers behind for them too!

YIELD: 7 TO 8 BARS OF SOAP (2.5 LBS/1.13 KG)

8.75 oz (248 g) distilled water

3.9 oz (111 g) sodium hydroxide (lye)

6 oz (170 g) coconut oil (21.4%)

5 oz (142 g) tallow or lard (17.9%)

1 tsp (2 g) propolis powder

14 oz (397 g) dandelion-infused olive oil (50%)

3 oz (85 g) sweet almond or sunflower oil (10.7%)

0.88 oz (25 g) lemongrass essential oil (optional)

Wearing protective gloves and eyewear, carefully stir the lye into the distilled water, then set the lye solution aside in a safe place to cool for about 30 to 40 minutes or until the temperature drops to around 100 to 110°F (38 to 43°C). Melt the coconut oil, tallow and propolis powder together, then add to the other oils, straining through a fine mesh stainless strainer first if you don't want a strongly speckled look from the propolis. Combine the warm oils with the cooled lye solution. Using a combination of hand stirring and an immersion blender, stir the soap until it reaches a light trace.

At trace, stir in the essential oil, if using, then pour into a prepared mold. Cover lightly with a sheet of wax or freezer paper, then a towel or light blanket. Peek at the soap every so often; if it starts developing a crack, move it to a cooler location. Keep the soap in the mold for 1 to 2 days, or until it's easy to remove, then slice it into bars when it's firm enough not to stick to your cutting tool. Cure on coated cooling racks or sheets of wax paper about 4 weeks before using.

TIP: Propolis powder can be purchased from health stores in bulk or as capsules that you can break apart before using. If you're using larger chunks of propolis directly from your beehives or local beekeeper, clean off any small pieces of debris, then freeze the propolis for several hours until solid. Run the solid chunks through a coffee grinder until powdered.

SUBSTITUTION: The 5 ounces (142 g) of tallow or lard can be replaced with 4 ounces (113 g) of cocoa or kokum butter plus 1 ounce (28 g) of castor oil instead. The lye amount will slightly reduce, down to 3.85 ounces (109 g).

Honey & Beeswax Soap

When added in small amounts, beeswax hardens soap, reduces the chance of soda ash (see page 184) and adds label appeal. Because a portion of it saponifies (turns into soap when mixed with lye), beeswax is usually calculated into recipes at around 0.5 to 3 percent. Be aware that more of a good thing isn't necessarily better in this case, as too much beeswax will reduce lather and make your soap feel draggy when rubbed across skin. Take special note of the higher temperatures required for this recipe and be prepared to work quickly. There's a learning curve when first working with beeswax, so it's suggested that you have a few successful batches of soap previously made before attempting this recipe.

YIELD: 7 TO 8 BARS OF SOAP (2.5 LBS/1.13 KG)

9 oz (255 g) distilled water

3.85 oz (109 g) sodium hydroxide (lye)

7 oz (198 g) coconut oil (25%)

0.5 oz (14 g) beeswax (1.8%)

15 oz (425 g) olive oil (53.6%)

4 oz (113 g) sweet almond oil (14.3%)

1.5 oz (43 g) castor oil (5.4%)

1 tsp (5 ml) honey mixed with 1 tsp (5 ml) warm water

1.06 oz (30 g) lavender essential oil (optional)

Wearing protective gloves and eyewear, carefully stir the lye into the distilled water, then set the lye solution aside in a safe place to cool until the temperature drops to around 125°F (52°C). For this recipe, you want to work with higher temperatures than normal. The oils should be around 145°F (63°C) and the lye solution around 125°F (52°C). Melt the coconut oil and beeswax completely, then add to the other oils. Combine the warm oils with the lye solution. Using a combination of hand stirring and an immersion blender, stir the soap until it reaches a light trace. Because of the higher temperatures and beeswax, this soap will likely reach trace in under 1 minute, so be prepared to work fast when that happens.

At trace, stir in the diluted honey and essential oil, if using, then immediately pour into a prepared loaf mold. If the room temperature is warm enough, you may not need to cover this soap. If the room temperature is cooler, or to ensure full gel phase, cover lightly with a sheet of wax or freezer paper, then a towel or light blanket. Peek at the soap every so often; if it starts developing a crack, uncover and move it to a cooler location. Keep the soap in the mold for 1 to 2 days, or until it's easy to remove, then slice it into bars when it's firm enough not to stick to your cutting tool. Cure on coated cooling racks or sheets of wax paper about 4 weeks before using.

> SUBSTITUTION: You can replace coconut oil in equal measure with babassu oil instead. The lye amount will decrease slightly to 3.8 ounces (108 g).

Orange Honey Shampoo Bars

These zesty shampoo bars are scented with a spritely blend of citrus essential oils that not only gives them a wonderful smell, but a small boost of cleansing power as well. Mango butter conditions hair while the natural humectant properties of honey add extra moisture and shine. If you don't have rice bran oil, you can use an equal amount of olive oil in its place, with no other changes needed. Like most shampoo bars, there's a generous amount of castor oil added to the recipe to ensure a great lathering experience.

YIELD: 7 TO 8 BARS OF SOAP (2.5 LBS/1.13 KG)

8.75 oz (248 g) distilled water

3.9 oz (111 g) sodium hydroxide (lye)

8 oz (227 g) coconut oil (28.6%)

3 oz (85 g) mango or shea butter (10.7%)

10 oz (283 g) rice bran oil (35.7%)

3 oz (85 g) sunflower or sweet almond oil (10.7%)

4 oz (113 g) castor oil (14.3%)

1 tsp (5 ml) honey mixed with 1 tsp (5 ml) warm water

0.88 oz (25 g) orange essential oil (use a folded or Valencia type)

0.35 oz (10 g) grapefruit essential oil

0.18 oz (5 g) litsea or lemongrass essential oil (about 1³/₄ tsp)

Wearing protective gloves and eyewear, carefully stir the lye into the distilled water, then set the lye solution aside in a safe place to cool for about 30 to 40 minutes or until the temperature drops to around 100 to 110°F (38 to 43°C). Melt the coconut oil and mango butter completely, then add to the other oils. Combine the warm oils with the lye solution. Using a combination of hand stirring and an immersion blender, stir the soap until it reaches a light trace.

At trace, stir in the diluted honey and essential oils, then pour into a prepared loaf mold. Cover lightly with a sheet of wax or freezer paper, then a towel or light blanket. Peek at the soap every so often; if it starts developing a crack, uncover and move it to a cooler location. Keep the soap in the mold for 1 to 2 days, or until it's easy to remove, then slice it into bars when it's firm enough not to stick to your cutting tool. Cure on coated cooling racks or sheets of wax paper about 4 weeks before using.

SUBSTITUTION: You can replace coconut oil in equal measure with babassu oil instead. The lye amount will decrease slightly to 3.85 ounces (109 g).

Bee Pollen & Honey Soap

An amazing superfood, bee pollen is packed with amino acids, vitamins, minerals, trace elements, protein and enzymes. It's incorporated into soaps and skin care products for its anti-inflammatory properties and to soften and smooth skin. Honey is valued as an ingredient for its moisturizing properties and as a lather booster. Cocoa butter is included in the recipe for increased hardness and a creamy feel in the final soap bars, but can be replaced with tallow or lard if desired. Because of the honey and bee pollen, this soap will overheat more easily than other recipes and will darken to a warm caramel brown if it goes through gel phase. To keep the lighter color shown, individual molds are recommended. Place the filled mold(s) in the refrigerator immediately after pouring to prevent gel phase (see page 21).

YIELD: 7 TO 8 BARS OF SOAP (2.5 LBS/1.13 KG)

8.75 oz (248 g) distilled water

3.95 oz (112 g) sodium hydroxide (lye)

8 oz (227 g) coconut oil (28.6%)

4 oz (113 g) cocoa or kokum butter (14.3%)

12 oz (340 g) olive oil (42.9%)

4 oz (113 g) sunflower or sweet almond oil (14.3%)

1½ tsp (7.5 ml) honey mixed with 1½ tsp (7.5 ml) warm water

1½ tsp (3.75 g) finely ground bee pollen powder

Wearing protective gloves and eyewear, carefully stir the lye into the distilled water, then set the lye solution aside in a safe place to cool for about 30 to 40 minutes or until the temperature drops to around 100 to 110°F (38 to 43°C). Melt the coconut oil and cocoa butter, then add to the other oils. Combine the warm oils with the lye solution. Using a combination of hand stirring and an immersion blender, stir the soap until it reaches trace.

At trace, stir in the diluted honey and bee pollen powder, then pour into individual molds or a prepared loaf mold. Immediately place the filled mold(s) in the refrigerator for 12 to 24 hours. Remove and return to room temperature. Don't try to unmold yet as the soap will be soft for another day or two. Cure the finished soaps on coated cooling racks or sheets of wax paper for at least 4 weeks before using.

SUBSTITUTION: Try using lard or tallow instead of the cocoa or kokum butter. The lye amount will stay within an acceptable range for either change and will not need to be adjusted.

Wild Rosehips & Honey Soap

This pretty pink soap gets its natural color from madder root, an heirloom dye plant. It's infused with rosehips, for their beneficial fruit acids and antioxidants, and rosehip seed oil for its naturally high in skin-regenerative compounds. Honey softens and moisturizes skin while enhancing the finished soap's lather. Shea butter nourishes and moisturizes while sweet almond oil conditions skin. For a rose-like aroma, the soap is primarily scented with geranium essential oil, but you may wish to leave it unscented or try another essential oil blend (see page 155).

YIELD: 7 TO 8 BARS OF SOAP (2.5 LBS/1.13 KG)

½ cup (55 g) rosehips (dried or fresh)

10 oz (283 g) distilled water

3.85 oz (109 g) sodium hydroxide (lye)

6 oz (170 g) coconut oil (21.4%)

3 oz (85 g) shea or mango butter (10.7%)

4 oz (113 g) sweet almond or sunflower oil (14.3%)

14 oz (397 g) olive oil (50%)

1 oz (28 g) rosehip seed oil (3.6%)

3½ tsp (6 g) madder root powder

1½ tsp (7.5 ml) honey mixed with 1½ tsp (7.5 ml) water

0.88 oz (25 g) geranium essential oil

0.35 oz (10 g) clary sage or lavender essential oil (optional)

FOR THE ROSEHIP TEA

Bring the distilled water to a boil in a small saucepan. Add the rosehips, cover and reduce heat to low. Simmer for 1 hour. Strain through a fine mesh sieve, mashing the rosehips to get as much juice as possible. Cool in the refrigerator until thoroughly chilled. Weigh out 8.75 ounces (248 g) of rosehip tea, adding more distilled water if needed.

FOR THE ROSEHIPS AND HONEY SOAP

Wearing protective gloves and eyewear, carefully stir the lye into the 8.75 ounces (248 g) of chilled rosehip tea, and then set the lye solution aside in a safe place to cool for about 30 to 40 minutes or until the temperature drops to around 100 to 110°F (38 to 43°C). Melt the coconut oil and shea butter, then add to the other oils. Stir the madder root into the warmed oils. Combine the oils and madder root mixture with the lye solution. Using a combination of hand stirring and an immersion blender, stir the soap until it reaches a light trace.

At trace, stir in the diluted honey and essential oils, then pour into a prepared mold or individual molds. Cover lightly with a sheet of wax or freezer paper, then a towel or light blanket. Peek at the soap every so often; if it starts developing a crack, uncover and move it to a cooler location. Keep the soap in the mold for 1 to 2 days, or until it's easy to remove, then slice it into bars when it's firm enough not to stick to your cutting tool. Cure on coated cooling racks or sheets of wax paper about 4 weeks before using.

SUBSTITUTION: To replace the shea or mango butter, try using lard or tallow instead. The lye amount will stay within an acceptable range for either change and will not need to be adjusted.

Soaps from the Forest

Featuring fresh woodsy scents such as cedarwood, fir needle and cypress, these soaps are perfect for those who enjoy spending time outdoors in nature.

Like splashing in a cold creek, Fir Needle & Mint Shampoo & Body Bars (page 119) cool and refresh while gently cleansing hair. Don't feel limited to just using it on the top of your head though, it makes a terrific all-over body soap too.

If you're looking for a unique handmade gift idea for the bearded men in your life, look no further than my Mountain Man Beard, Shampoo & Body Bar recipe (page 126). Every rugged guy that tries this soap gives it two big thumbs-ups!

For fans of old-fashioned favorites, I've included a recipe for Pine Tar Soap (page 129), a remedy from yesteryear, valued in the treatment of skin conditions such as psoriasis and eczema.

Fir Needle & Mint Shampoo & Body Bars

These shampoo bars gently wash away dirt while invigorating the senses with a cool refreshing essential oil blend. Jojoba oil adds shine and conditions hair while coconut and castor oils team up for a satisfying lathering experience. Shampoo bars often work best when followed by a vinegar rinse, especially if you have hard water that tends to leave mineral residues. The vinegar restores hair's pH while washing away soapy buildup. To make a vinegar rinse, combine equal parts vinegar and water, pour the combination over your hair after washing with a shampoo bar and rinse well.

YIELD: 7 TO 8 BARS OF SOAP (2.5 LBS/1.13 KG)

8.75 oz (248 g) distilled water

3.8 oz (108 g) sodium hydroxide (lye)

8 oz (227 g) coconut oil (28.6%)

10 oz (283 g) olive oil (35.7%)

4 oz (113 g) sunflower or sweet almond oil (14.3%)

4 oz (113 g) castor oil (14.3%)

2 oz (57 g) jojoba oil (7.1%)

0.53 oz (15 g) peppermint essential oil

0.42 oz (12 g) lavender essential oil

0.28 oz (8 g) fir needle essential oil

Wearing protective gloves and eyewear, carefully stir the lye into the distilled water, then set the lye solution aside in a safe place to cool for about 30 to 40 minutes or until the temperature drops to around 100 to 110°F (38 to 43°C). Melt the coconut oil, then add to the other oils. Combine the warm oils with the lye solution. Using a combination of hand stirring and an immersion blender, stir the soap until it reaches a light trace.

At trace, stir in the essential oils and pour into a prepared loaf mold. Cover lightly with a sheet of wax or freezer paper, then a towel or light blanket. Peek at the soap every so often; if it starts developing a crack, uncover and move it to a cooler location. Keep the soap in the mold for 1 to 2 days, or until it's easy to remove, then slice it into bars when it's firm enough not to stick to your cutting tool. Cure on coated cooling racks or sheets of wax paper about 4 weeks before using.

SUBSTITUTION: If jojoba oil isn't available, try hemp or avocado oil in its place. The lye amount will increase to 3.9 ounces (111 g).

Zesty Juniper Berry & Orange Soap

Dried juniper berries are a wonderful earthy addition to soap and are valued especially for use by those who tend towards oily skin and breakouts. In this recipe, the berries are ground into a powder and incorporated in the lye solution, while several more embellish the soap's top. The intoxicating fragrance derives from a warm blend of orange, juniper and patchouli essential oils. Remember that regular orange essential oil will quickly fade from soap, so look for the concentrated, folded versions such as 5× (five-fold) or 10× (ten-fold).

YIELD: 7 TO 8 BARS OF SOAP (2.5 LBS/1.13 KG)

½ tbsp (3 g) dried juniper berries

8.75 oz (248 g) distilled water

3.9 oz (111 g) sodium hydroxide (lye)

7 oz (198 g) coconut oil (25%)

15.5 oz (439 g) olive oil (55.4%)

4 oz (113 g) sunflower or sweet almond oil (14.3%)

1.5 oz (43 g) castor oil (5.3%)

0.56 oz (16 g) orange essential oil (a folded type or Valencia orange)

0.28 oz (8 g) juniper essential oil

0.21 oz (6 g) patchouli essential oil (about 2 tsp)

Extra juniper berries, for decoration

Place the dried juniper berries in a coffee grinder and process until evenly powdered. Set aside while you prepare the lye solution.

Wearing protective gloves and eyewear, carefully stir the lye into the distilled water. Stir the ground juniper berries into the lye solution, then set it aside in a safe place to cool for about 30 to 40 minutes or until the temperature drops to around 100 to 110°F (38 to 43°C). Melt the coconut oil, then add to the other oils. Combine the warm oils with the lye solution. Using a combination of hand stirring and an immersion blender, stir the soap until it reaches a light trace.

At trace, stir in the essential oils and pour into a prepared loaf mold. If desired, top the soap with whole juniper berries and extra ground juniper berry powder before covering lightly with a sheet of wax or freezer paper, then a towel or light blanket. Peek at the soap every so often; if it starts developing a crack, uncover and move it to a cooler location. Keep the soap in the mold for 1 to 2 days, or until it's easy to remove, then slice it into bars when it's firm enough not to stick to your cutting tool. Cure on coated cooling racks or sheets of wax paper about 4 weeks before using.

SUBSTITUTION: Coconut oil can be replaced in equal measure by babassu oil. The lye amount will slightly decrease to 3.85 ounces (109 g).

Classic Cedarwood & Coconut Milk Shave Soap

The best-lathering shave soaps are dual lye. That means they're made by combining sodium hydroxide, which is used to make solid bars of soap, with potassium hydroxide, used to make liquid soap. The added amount of potassium hydroxide ensures the soap lathers more easily. Shave soaps need to contain a great deal of stearic acid, which contributes to a dense creamy lather that's suitable for shaving. Unfortunately for palm-free soapmakers, commercially available stearic acid is usually derived from palm oil. Besides soy wax, a next best source of naturally occurring stearic acid is kokum butter, which is why you'll notice a high amount in this recipe. Olive oil is not required in shaving soap recipes; so don't be alarmed at its absence. This recipe differs significantly from others in this book in that it has a high water content and it must be cooked using a modified hot process method. Since this is an advanced technique, it's a good idea to have completed several successful batches of soap before attempting this recipe.

YIELD: 8 TO 10 ROUND BARS OF SHAVING SOAP (2 LBS 5 OZ/1.05 KG)

10 oz (283 g) distilled water

6 oz (170 g) coconut milk

1.2 oz (34 g) sodium hydroxide

1.8 oz (51 g) potassium hydroxide

10.6 oz (300 g) kokum butter (60%)

3.5 oz (100 g) coconut oil (20%)

2.6 oz (75 g) castor oil (15%)

0.88 oz (25 g) shea butter (5%)

0.5 oz (14 g) vegetable glycerin

0.18 oz (5 g) cedarwood Atlas essential oil (about 1½ tsp)

0.07 oz (2 g) clove essential oil (about ⅝ tsp) (optional)

0.07 oz (2 g) vetiver essential oil (about ¾ tsp) (optional)

Shaving brush, required for proper lathering

Combine the distilled water and coconut milk. Wearing protective gloves and eyewear, carefully stir both types of lye into the combined water and milk mixture until completely dissolved. Set the lye solution aside to cool slightly while preparing the butters and oils. Melt the butters and coconut oil, then add them with the castor oil into a 2 quart (1.89 L) slow cooker. Turn the slow cooker's heat to low. (See photo 1.)

Pour the lye solution into the warmed oils and start stirring, using a combination of hand stirring and an immersion blender until trace is reached. This may take anywhere from 3 to 10 minutes, depending on the type of the coconut milk used and temperature of the oils, lye solution and slow cooker. (See photo 2.)

Once trace is reached, cover the slow cooker and allow the soap to cook undisturbed, checking every 15 minutes to be sure it's not overflowing from the cooker and stirring as needed. The soap will go through several stages as it cooks, resembling a thin porridge that noticeably thickens over cook time. (See photos 3 to 5, which show the batter after 15 minutes, 30 minutes and 45 minutes.)

Liquid may pool up and separate from the soap batter while it cooks, but that's normal. After 45 minutes of cooking, remove the lid and stir the soap. After stirring, there will likely be visible lumps of soap forming in the otherwise liquid soap batter; this is normal. (See photo 6.)

(continued)

Classic Cedarwood & Coconut Milk Shave Soap (Cont.)

Cook the soap an additional 15 minutes or until it's transparent and resembles thick petroleum jelly or glossy mashed potatoes when stirred. To make sure it's fully cooked, remove a tiny bit of soap batter, let it cool to a comfortable temperature and dab just the tip of your tongue on it. If you feel a zapping sensation, similar to licking a battery, it needs to cook longer. If it just tastes like soap, it's fully cooked. Regardless of the outcome, be sure to rinse your mouth out thoroughly after this test. (See photo 7 before stirring, photo 8 after stirring.)

Turn the slow cooker off. In a small bowl, mix the vegetable glycerin and essential oils together. Stir this mixture into the still hot soap batter. The glycerin will help loosen the soap, making it easier to work with and helps promote a better lather once the soap is cured.

Spoon the soap batter into a silicone column mold or press it into individual round molds. The rounded shape makes it easier to fit inside a shaving mug or bowl. Leave the soap in the molds, uncovered, for 24 hours or until completely cool. Cure the soaps for at least 3 weeks before use, allowing excess water to evaporate out, yielding a harder bar with better lather. (See photo 9 spooning into the mold.)

TIP: To use shave soap, place the soap round in a small bowl or mug. Generously splash some water on the shaving brush and in the bowl/mug and start making a vigorous circular motion over the soap with your brush for a few minutes until a thick creamy lather forms.

VARIATION: For a fun floral variation, try adding 1 teaspoon (3.6 g) of rose or purple clay to the hot lye solution, for color, along with 0.17 (5 g) lavender or geranium essential oil. A shave brush will be required to work up the proper amount of lather.

Mountain Man Beard, Shampoo & Body Bars

In this recipe, hemp (or avocado) oil combines with shea butter to add extra moisturizing and conditioning properties for washing beards of all types. Castor and coconut oil ensures plenty of lather, while olive oil gently cleanses away dirt without drying the skin beneath. Nutrient-rich honey, along with a woodsy blend of essential oils, rounds out this soap's features. Coupled with a nourishing beard oil, these rugged beard bars would make the perfect gift for the bearded guy in your life.

YIELD: 7 TO 8 BARS OF SOAP (2.5 LBS/1.13 KG)

8.5 oz (241 g) distilled water

3.85 oz (109 g) sodium hydroxide (lye)

6.5 oz (184 g) coconut oil (23.2%)

2 oz (57 g) shea or mango butter (7.1%)

12 oz (340 g) olive oil (42.9%)

3.5 oz (99 g) hemp or avocado oil (12.5%)

4 oz (113 g) castor oil (14.3%)

1 tsp (5 ml) honey diluted with 1 tsp (5 ml) water (optional)

0.88 oz (25 g) cedarwood Atlas essential oil

0.18 oz (5 g) cypress essential oil (about 1³/₄ tsp)

0.18 oz (5 g) fir needle essential oil (about 1³/₄ tsp)

Wearing protective gloves and eyewear, carefully stir the lye into the distilled water, then set the lye solution aside in a safe place to cool for about 30 to 40 minutes or until the temperature drops to around 100 to 110°F (38 to 43°C). Melt the coconut oil and shea butter, then add to the other oils. Combine the warm oils with the lye solution. Using a combination of hand stirring and an immersion blender, stir the soap until it reaches a light trace.

At trace, stir in the diluted honey and essential oils, then pour into a prepared mold or individual molds. Cover lightly with a sheet of wax or freezer paper, then a towel or light blanket. Peek at the soap every so often; if it starts developing a crack, uncover and move it to a cooler location. Keep the soap in the mold for 1 to 2 days, or until it's easy to remove, then slice it into bars when it's firm enough not to stick to your cutting tool. Cure on coated cooling racks or sheets of wax paper. This bar starts out softer than most and will require a longer cure time of at least 6 to 8 weeks before using.

SUBSTITUTION: To replace the shea or mango butter, try using lard or tallow instead. The lye amount will stay within an acceptable range for either change and will not need to be adjusted.

Old Fashioned Pine Tar Soap

In days past, pine tar soaps were used in the treatment of skin conditions, such as eczema and psoriasis, while pine tar shampoos helped relieve itchy scalps and dandruff. These days, pine tar can usually be found in your local feed or farm store as it's used to treat horse's hooves. The scent from pine tar is quite strong during cure time, so you may want to cure this one in a separate area from your other soaps. The bold piney scent will remain in the soap for well over a year, appealing to those looking for a woodsy soap that lathers well as it leaves skin feeling clean and refreshed.

YIELD: 7 TO 8 BARS OF SOAP (2.5 LBS/1.13 KG)

9 oz (255 g) distilled water

3.55 oz (101 g) sodium hydroxide (lye)

7 oz (198 g) coconut oil (25%)

8 oz (227 g) tallow or lard (28.6%)

10 oz (283 g) olive oil (35.7%)

3 oz (85 g) pine tar (10.7%)

Wearing protective gloves and eyewear, carefully stir the lye into the distilled water, then set the lye solution aside in a safe place to cool for about 30 to 40 minutes or until the temperature drops to around 100 to 110°F (38 to 43°C). Melt the coconut oil and tallow, then add to the olive oil. Add the pine tar to the warm oils. Combine the oils and pine tar mixture with the lye solution. Pine tar soap tends to set up fast, so you may only need to hand stir it for a few minutes to reach trace.

At trace, pour into a prepared mold or individual molds. Cover lightly with a sheet of wax or freezer paper, then a towel or light blanket. Peek at the soap every so often; if it starts developing a crack, uncover and move it to a cooler location. Keep the soap in the mold for 1 to 2 days, or until it's easy to remove, then slice it into bars when it's firm enough not to stick to your cutting tool. Cure on coated cooling racks or sheets of wax paper about 4 weeks before using.

SUBSTITUTION: For a vegan variation, omit the 8 ounces (227 g) of tallow or lard. Replace that amount with a combination of 4 ounces (113 g) cocoa or kokum butter, 1.5 ounces (43 g) castor oil and 2.5 ounces (71 g) sunflower, avocado or sweet almond oil. The required lye amount will slightly decrease to 3.5 ounces (99 g).

Lumberjack Soap

Boasting an earthy woodsy scent, this soap is a favorite with everyone who tries it. It's naturally colored with a combination of chlorella and sage powders and scented with a forest-inspired blend of cedarwood, clove and vetiver essential oils. The saturated fats in tallow (or lard) are incredibly beneficial and moisturizing for skin. Check the substitution box below if you're seeking a vegan alternative.

YIELD: 7 TO 8 BARS OF SOAP (2.5 LBS/1.13 KG)

8.5 oz (241 g) distilled water

3.85 oz (109 g) sodium hydroxide (lye)

1 tsp (4 g) chlorella powder

1 tsp (1 g) sage powder

6 oz (170 g) coconut oil (21.4%)

4 oz (113 g) tallow or lard (14.3%)

10 oz (283 g) olive oil (35.7%)

6 oz (170 g) rice bran oil (21.5%)

2 oz (57 g) castor oil (7.1%)

0.99 oz (28 g) cedarwood Atlas essential oil

0.14 oz (4 g) clove essential oil (about 1¼ tsp)

0.14 oz (4 g) vetiver essential oil (about 1⅜ tsp)

Wearing protective gloves and eyewear, carefully stir the lye into the distilled water. Stir in the chlorella and sage powders, then set the lye solution aside in a safe place to cool for about 30 to 40 minutes or until the temperature drops to around 100 to 110°F (38 to 43°C). Melt the coconut oil and tallow (or lard), then add to the other oils. Combine the warm oils with the lye solution. Using a combination of hand stirring and an immersion blender, stir the soap until it reaches a light trace.

At trace, stir in the essential oils then pour into a prepared mold or individual molds. Cover lightly with a sheet of wax or freezer paper, then a towel or light blanket. Peek at the soap every so often; if it starts developing a crack, uncover and move it to a cooler location. Keep the soap in the mold for 1 to 2 days, or until it's easy to remove, then slice it into bars when it's firm enough not to stick to your cutting tool. Cure on coated cooling racks or sheets of wax paper about 4 weeks before using.

SUBSTITUTION: To replace the tallow or lard, try using cocoa or kokum butter instead. The lye amount will stay within an acceptable range for either change and will not need to be adjusted.

Soaps from the Spa

Filled with mineral-rich clays, luxurious butters and touches of silk, the recipes in this section revolve around spa favorites, along with a few specialty soaps thrown in.

If you love products with skin-soothing cucumbers, you're going to adore Cucumber and Charcoal Swirl Soap on page 136. It features a zeolite clay that naturally draws impurities from the surface of your skin, leaving it clean and glowing.

Rooibos tea drinkers will be pleased to learn that their favorite beverage is also a powerful skin soother. Combined with ancient rhassoul clay, it forms the basis of Soothing Red Rooibos & Rhassoul Clay Soap, page 139, which thoroughly cleans even the most sensitive skin without stripping valuable moisture.

Coffee and cocoa lovers will absolutely fall in love with the Mocha Coffee Bean Scrub Bar, page 140. Filled with real coffee beans, cocoa powder and richly scented natural cocoa butter, it's a delightfully indulgent treat for the senses!

Regenerating French Clay & Yogurt Soap

Rich in minerals, the color in French green clay comes from a naturally occurring mixture of iron oxides and decomposed plant matter. This beautiful clay pulls impurities from deep within pores, leaving your complexion fresh and revitalized, while lactic acid and other beneficial compounds in yogurt smoothes and rejuvenates. A generous helping of avocado oil provides nourishing essential fatty acids, but if that's not available or you're allergic, try hempseed oil for a similar effect. Since this soap is suited for delicate facial skin or sensitive complexions, I prefer leaving it unscented, though you're free to add essential oils, if desired. (See page 155 for essential oil blend ideas.)

YIELD: 7 TO 8 BARS OF SOAP (2.5 LBS/1.13 KG)

8 oz (227 g) distilled water

3.85 oz (109 g) sodium hydroxide (lye)

3 tsp (13 g) French green clay

6.5 oz (184 g) coconut oil (23.2%)

3.5 oz (99 g) mango or shea butter (12.5%)

12 oz (340 g) olive oil (42.9%)

4.5 oz (128 g) avocado oil (16%)

1.5 oz (43 g) castor oil (5.4%)

1 oz (28 g) plain unsweetened yogurt

Wearing protective gloves and eyewear, carefully stir the lye into the distilled water. Stir in the French green clay, then set the lye solution aside in a safe place to cool for about 30 to 40 minutes or until the temperature drops to around 100 to 110°F (38 to 43°C). Melt the coconut oil and mango butter, then add to the other oils. Thoroughly blend the yogurt with the warm oils using an immersion blender. Add the lye solution. Using a combination of hand stirring and an immersion blender, stir the soap until it reaches a light trace.

At trace, pour into a prepared mold or individual molds. Cover lightly with a sheet of wax or freezer paper, then a towel or light blanket. Peek at the soap every so often; if it starts developing a crack, uncover and move it to a cooler location. Keep the soap in the mold for 1 to 2 days, or until it's easy to remove, then slice it into bars when it's firm enough not to stick to your cutting tool. Cure on coated cooling racks or sheets of wax paper about 4 weeks before using.

SUBSTITUTION: To replace the mango or shea butter, try using lard or tallow instead. The lye amount will stay within an acceptable range for either change and will not need to be adjusted.

Cucumber & Charcoal Swirl Soap

A cooling skincare favorite, cucumbers are loaded with nutrients and beneficial compounds to revitalize and brighten your skin. Green zeolite clay is prized for its ability to absorb toxins and impurities and adds a lovely natural color and light texture to handmade soap. In this recipe, I stirred activated charcoal into a portion of the soap batter, creating a simple swirl design. (See page 177 for more on making swirls in soap.) Alternatively, you could create a layered soap instead. Because this soap is high in olive oil, it may take a week or two longer to firm up and cure than other soaps. Your patience will be rewarded, however, with a soap that's extra gentle and mild. For a hint of fresh mint scent, I added a small amount of spearmint essential oil to this recipe, but you may want to leave it unscented, especially if the soap is intended for someone with sensitive skin.

YIELD: 7 TO 8 BARS OF SOAP (2.5 LBS/1.13 KG)

3.5 oz (99 g) fresh cucumber, cut into slices

2 oz (57 g) distilled water

About 4 oz (113 g) of additional distilled water

3.85 oz (109 g) sodium hydroxide (lye)

2 tsp (10 g) green zeolite clay

6 oz (170 g) coconut oil (21.4%)

16.5 oz (454 g) olive oil (59%)

4 oz (113 g) hemp oil (14.3%)

1.5 oz (43 g) castor oil (5.4%)

¼ tsp activated charcoal powder mixed with 2 tsp (10 ml) water

0.70 oz (20 g) spearmint essential oil (optional)

SUBSTITUTION: If green zeolite clay is unavailable, try another type of clay instead such as French green clay, Cambrian blue clay or rose kaolin clay, for a different look.

TO MAKE THE CUCUMBER JUICE

Using a blender or food processor, blend the cucumber slices and 2 ounces (57 g) of distilled water together. Press through a strainer to remove seeds and large pieces. Add enough additional distilled water to the cucumber juice until it totals 8.75 ounces (248 g). Store in the refrigerator until needed, or up to 2 days.

TO MAKE THE SOAP

Wearing protective gloves and eyewear, carefully stir the lye into the 8.75 ounces (248 g) of chilled cucumber juice. It's normal for the lye solution to turn a shade of yellow or yellow-green. Stir in the green zeolite clay, then set the lye solution aside in a safe place to cool for about 30 to 40 minutes or until the temperature drops to around 100 to 110°F (38 to 43°C). Melt the coconut oil, then add to the other oils. Combine the warm oils with the lye solution. Using a combination of hand stirring and an immersion blender, stir the soap until it reaches a light trace.

At trace, stir in the essential oil, if using. Weigh and separate out around one-third, or 13 ounces (369 g), of soap batter and stir the diluted activated charcoal into it. Leave the remaining soap batter plain. Following the directions on page 177, swirl the two colors together in a prepared mold. Cover lightly with a sheet of wax or freezer paper, then a towel or light blanket. Peek at the soap every so often; if it starts developing a crack, uncover and move it to a cooler location. Keep the soap in the mold for 1 to 2 days, or until it's easy to remove, then slice it into bars when it's firm enough not to stick to your cutting tool. Cure on coated cooling racks or sheets of wax paper at least 4 to 5 weeks before using.

Soothing Red Rooibos & Rhassoul Clay Soap

An ancient clay, Rhassoul is a spa favorite because of its fantastic ability to gently purify even the most sensitive skin types. It's stellar in hair care recipes too, leaving locks clean and shiny. In this soap recipe, I combined it with a small amount of rose kaolin clay so the finished soap is pink-toned, instead of the brown color it would otherwise end up. Rooibos tea is prized for its abundance of natural antioxidants and alpha hydroxy acids, along with its use in soothing irritated or inflamed skin conditions. Geranium essential oil was added to this recipe for its rosy scent and because it can be helpful for balancing most skin types, but lavender essential oil would also be lovely in this soap.

YIELD: 7 TO 8 BARS OF SOAP (2.5 LBS/1.13 KG)

1 tsp (3 g) red rooibos tea leaves

9 oz (255 g) distilled water, divided

3.9 oz (111 g) sodium hydroxide (lye)

2 tsp (12.6 g) rhassoul clay

1 tsp (3 g) rose kaolin clay

7 oz (198 g) coconut oil (25%)

14 oz (397 g) olive oil (50%)

3.5 oz (99 g) sunflower oil (12.5%)

3 oz (85 g) apricot kernel oil (10.7%)

0.5 oz (14 g) castor oil (1.8%)

0.88 oz (25 g) geranium essential oil (optional)

TO MAKE THE RED ROOIBOS TEA

Place the tea leaves in a heat-proof cup or mug. Bring 4 ounces (113 g) of distilled water to a simmer then pour over the tea. Steep for 10 minutes, strain and chill for several hours before using.

TO MAKE THE SOAP

Weigh the amount of chilled tea and add additional distilled water until you have 8.75 ounces (248 g) total liquid for making the recipe. Wearing protective gloves and eyewear, carefully stir the lye into the tea mixture. Stir in the rhassoul and pink kaolin clays until dissolved, then set the lye solution aside in a safe place to cool for about 30 to 40 minutes or until the temperature drops to around 100 to 110°F (38 to 43°C). Melt the coconut oil, then add to the other oils. Combine the warm oils with the lye solution. Using a combination of hand stirring and an immersion blender, stir the soap until it reaches a light trace.

At trace, stir in the essential oil, if using, then pour into a prepared mold or individual molds. Cover lightly with a sheet of wax or freezer paper, then a towel or light blanket. Peek at the soap every so often; if it starts developing a crack, uncover and move it to a cooler location. Keep the soap in the mold for 1 to 2 days, or until it's easy to remove, then slice it into bars when it's firm enough not to stick to your cutting tool. Cure on coated cooling racks or sheets of wax paper about 4 weeks before using.

SUBSTITUTION: Apricot kernel oil is especially good for sensitive skin, but if it's not available, it can be replaced with sweet almond, hemp or avocado oil. If using a dark green unrefined hemp or avocado oil, be aware that its natural green color will mix with the rose clay, creating a muddy color. In this case, you may wish to omit the rose clay completely.

Mocha Coffee Bean Scrub Bars

If you adore the combination of coffee and chocolate, then this is the soap you need in your life! Unrefined cocoa butter contributes a wonderful chocolate aroma, while cocoa powder adds a warm brown color. Scrubs made with ground coffee beans are an oft-used beauty trick for temporarily reducing the appearance of cellulite, but this soap can be used as an all-over body bar as well. Kukui nut oil adds a luxurious touch, but if it's not available, see the substitution options below for alternatives. Coffee essential oil gives this soap a delicious jolt of fresh coffee scent, but can be omitted if it's difficult to obtain.

YIELD: 7 TO 8 BARS OF SOAP (2.5 LBS/1.13 KG)

8.75 oz (248 g) strong brewed coffee, chilled

3.9 oz (111 g) sodium hydroxide (lye)

7 oz (198 g) coconut oil (25%)

4 oz (113 g) unrefined cocoa butter (14.3%)

12 oz (340 g) olive oil (42.9%)

3 oz (85 g) sweet almond oil (10.7%)

2 oz (57 g) kukui nut oil (7.1%)

0.88 oz (25 g) coffee essential oil (optional)

2 tsp (3 g) used coffee grounds

1 tsp (2 g) cocoa powder

Extra cocoa powder for making a pencil line, optional

Whole coffee beans for decoration, optional

Wearing protective gloves and eyewear, carefully stir the lye into the chilled coffee. It's normal for the lye solution to turn brown. It may also have a temporarily unpleasant aroma, but it won't last. Set the lye solution aside in a safe place to cool for about 30 to 40 minutes or until the temperature drops to around 100 to 110°F (38 to 43°C). Melt the coconut oil and cocoa butter, then add to the other oils. Combine the warm oils with the lye solution. Using a combination of hand stirring and an immersion blender, stir the soap until it reaches a light trace.

Stir in the coffee essential oil. Divide the soap batter equally. In one half of the soap batter, stir in the coffee grounds and cocoa powder until well blended. Leave the other half of the soap batter plain.

Following the directions on page 170, pour the soap batter with the coffee grounds and cocoa powder into the bottom of a prepared mold. If you'd like to make a pencil line between the layers, lightly sprinkle cocoa powder over the first layer. (See page 173 for more on making pencil lines in soap.) Next, pour the plain layer of soap. If desired, decorate the top of the soap with whole coffee beans and/or extra coffee grounds.

Keep the soap in the mold for 1 to 2 days, or until it's easy to remove, then slice it into bars when it's firm enough not to stick to your cutting tool. Cure on coated cooling racks or sheets of wax paper about 4 weeks before using.

SUBSTITUTION: Kukui nut oil can be replaced with sunflower, avocado or more olive oil. The lye amount will stay within an acceptable range with any of these changes and will not need to be adjusted.

Triple Butter Silk & Agave Soap

This sumptuous soap is brimming with ingredients that your skin will adore. A trio of creamy conditioning butters ensures that your skin is well nourished, while silk adds an unparalleled touch of luxury. The natural sugars from agave syrup provides a small boost to lather, but if it's not available, honey can be used in its place. While I chose to scent this soap simply with lavender essential oil, you could also consider one of the essential oil combinations or blends listed on page 155.

YIELD: 7 TO 8 BARS OF SOAP (2.5 LBS/1.13 KG)

8.75 oz (248 g) distilled water

3.85 oz (109 g) sodium hydroxide (lye)

Small pinch of Tussah silk

7 oz (198 g) coconut oil (25%)

3 oz (85 g) cocoa butter (10.7%)

3 oz (85 g) mango butter (10.7%)

3 oz (85 g) shea butter (10.7%)

12 oz (340 g) olive oil (42.9%)

1 tsp (5 ml) agave syrup mixed with 1 tsp (5 ml) water

1.23 oz (35 g) lavender essential oil (optional)

Wearing protective gloves and eyewear, carefully stir the lye into the distilled water. Add a small pinch of silk, then stir thoroughly. Set the lye solution aside in a safe place to cool. Melt the coconut oil and solid butters, then add to the olive oil. Add the lye solution to the warm oils. Using a combination of hand stirring and an immersion blender, stir the soap until it reaches a light trace.

Stir in the essential oil, if using, and diluted agave syrup. Pour the soap batter into a prepared mold or individual molds. Cover lightly with a sheet of wax or freezer paper, then a towel or light blanket. Peek at the soap every so often; if it starts developing a crack, uncover and move it to a cooler location. Keep the soap in the mold for 1 to 2 days, or until it's easy to remove, then slice it into bars when it's firm enough not to stick to your cutting tool. Cure on coated cooling racks or sheets of wax paper about 4 weeks before using.

Part 3

Techniques & Tips to Take Your Soapmaking to the Next Level

In this section we'll explore exciting topics such as using natural colorants and essential oils to better personalize your soap recipes. You'll also learn how to infuse herbs, flowers and other plants into oils, teas and milks to enrich your soaps with their beneficial compounds.

You'll discover all sorts of interesting ingredients you can stir into your soap recipes from aloe and cranberry seeds to cornmeal and silk.

I'll share tricks for making the tops of your soaps pretty and how to add simple layers and swirl designs. You'll learn how a basic baking mat found in your local craft store can turn a loaf of soap into a beautiful work of art, with very little extra effort needed.

In short, this chapter is all about expanding your soapmaking skills and having fun while you do so!

TIPS FOR WORKING WITH NATURAL SOAP COLORANTS

There are a few important things to remember when working with natural colorants.

Because they're nature-derived and not mass-manufactured, colors and properties can vary depending on harvest and supplier. Adding to the confusion, the same colorant can, sometimes drastically, differ in how it presents in soap, depending on what stage it's added to a recipe and even whether it's mixed with oil or water first.

This makes working with natural colorants something of a wild card. For this reason, keep in mind that the photo gallery of natural colorants, starting on page 146 in this book, is meant to give a reasonable idea of what color you can expect, but not a guarantee.

For best results, use light colored oils in your soaps containing added natural colorants. Oils that are naturally tinted dark green, such as extra virgin olive oil and unrefined avocado and hempseed oil, will influence the color of the soap. This can be a positive when working with natural green colorants such as chlorella and French green clay, but the green tint can muddy other colorants such as rose or purple clay.

Be careful with herbal water infusions too, as teas that are allowed to steep too long will turn soap shades of tan to dark brown. Some examples that should not steep too long include lavender buds, rose petals and mint leaves.

Natural colorants tend to show up more brightly when soap is allowed to go through gel phase (see page 21). For some, like alkanet root, gel phase is almost imperative to develop a good color, but others, like clays, are less fussy.

Natural colorants tend to fade over time. One of their biggest drawbacks is that they lose color faster than their synthetic counterparts. Some, like matcha green tea, will turn from green to brown within a matter of days, while others, like colored clays, will stick around for the life of the soap. For the best odds of color longevity, keep soaps with natural colorants out of sunlight. Make small batches to use up within a few months, while the colors are still bright and pretty.

PHOTO GALLERY OF NATURAL SOAP COLORANTS

Over the next several pages, you'll find a gallery showcasing a variety of naturally colored soaps. Unless otherwise noted, soaps have cured at least 2 months. PPO means "per pound (454 g) of oils."

2 tsp rose clay PPO,
added to lye solution

1 tsp rose clay PPO,
added to lye solution

$1/2$ tsp rose clay PPO,
added to lye solution

2 tsp madder root PPO,
added to oils

1 tsp madder root PPO,
added to oils

$1/2$ tsp madder root PPO,
added to oils

1 tsp madder root PPO,
stirred with oil &
added at trace

1 tsp madder root PPO,
stirred with water
& added at trace

1 tsp madder root PPO,
added to lye solution

2 tsp red Brazilian clay PPO, stirred with water & added at trace

¼ tsp Australia red clay PPO, added to lye solution

1 tsp aloe leaf powder PPO, added to lye solution

1 tsp turkey rhubarb root powder PPO, added to oils

½ tsp turkey rhubarb root powder PPO, added to oils

½ tsp yellow dock powder PPO, added to lye solution

1 tsp buckthorn bark powder PPO, added to lye solution

1 tsp red Moroccan clay PPO, added to lye solution

2 tsp Egyptian pink clay PPO, added to lye solution

2 tbsp tomato paste PPO, blended with oils

2 tsp paprika PPO, added to lye solution

1 tsp paprika PPO, added to lye solution

2 tsp yellow Brazilian clay PPO, added to lye solution

1 oz sea buckthorn oil PPO, replaces 1 oz of olive oil in recipe

2 tsp annatto seed powder PPO, stirred into oils

2 tsp annatto seed powder PPO, added to lye solution

1/2 tsp annatto seed powder PPO, added to lye solution

1/2 tsp annatto seed powder PPO, added to oils

carrot juice as a full replacement for distilled water

¼ tsp saffron powder PPO, added to oils

¼ tsp saffron powder PPO, added to lye solution

½ tsp yellow French clay PPO, added to lye solution

1 tsp grapefruit peel powder PPO, added to lye solution

1 tsp orange peel powder PPO, added to oils

1 tsp orange peel powder PPO, added to lye solution

1 tsp lemon peel powder PPO, added to lye solution

1 tsp lemon peel powder PPO, added to oils

1 tsp wheatgrass powder PPO, added to lye solution

1 tsp barley powder PPO, added to lye solution

1 tsp oatstraw powder PPO, added to lye solution

1 tsp oatstraw powder PPO, added to oils

1 tsp parsley powder PPO, added to oils

1 tsp parsley powder PPO, added to lye solution

2 tsp alfalfa powder PPO, added to lye solution

2 tsp alfalfa powder PPO, added to oils

$\frac{1}{2}$ tsp safflower powder PPO, added to oils

1 tsp spirulina PPO,
added to oils (after
2 week cure)

1 tsp spirulina PPO,
stirred with oil & added
at trace

1 tsp spirulina PPO,
added to oils (after
2 month cure)

1 tsp spirulina PPO,
added to lye solution
(after 2 week cure)

1 tsp spirulina PPO,
added to lye solution
(after 2 month cure)

1 tsp chlorella PPO,
added to oils (after
2 week cure)

1 tsp chlorella PPO,
added to oils (after
2 month cure)

1 tsp chlorella PPO,
stirred with water &
added at trace (after
2 week cure)

1 tsp chlorella PPO,
stirred with water &
added at trace (after
2 month cure)

1 tbsp liquid chlorophyll PPO, added at trace

2 tsp green zeolite clay PPO, added to lye solution

1 tsp mugwort powder PPO, stirred in at trace

3 tsp French green clay PPO, added to lye solution

1 tsp French green clay PPO, added to lye solution

2 tsp chickweed powder PPO, added to oils

1 tsp moringa powder PPO, added to oils

1 tsp moringa powder PPO, added to lye solution

1 oz laurel berry fruit oil PPO, replaces 1 oz of olive oil in a recipe

1½ tsp woad PPO, added
to lye solution

1 tsp woad PPO, added to
oils

1 tsp woad PPO, mixed
with oil & added at trace

1 tsp woad PPO, mixed
with hot water &
added at trace

1 tsp woad PPO, added
to lye solution

½ tsp woad PPO, added to
lye solution

3 tsp Cambrian blue
clay PPO, added to lye
solution

1½ tsp Cambrian blue
clay PPO, added to lye
solution

1 tsp Cambrian blue
clay PPO, added to lye
solution

1½ tsp indigo PPO, added to lye solution

1 tsp indigo PPO, added to lye solution

½ tsp indigo PPO, added to lye solution

1 tsp indigo PPO, added to oils

1 tsp indigo PPO, mixed with oil & added at trace

1 tsp indigo PPO, mixed with hot water & added at trace

½ tsp alkanet root powder PPO, added to oils

½ tsp gromwell root powder PPO, added to oils

2 tsp purple Brazilian clay PPO, added to lye solution

ESSENTIAL OILS & USAGE RATES IN SOAP

If you'd like to add scent to your soap and keep it all natural, essential oils are the best way to do so. Unlike fragrance oils, which are made from a combination of synthetic and natural compounds, essential oils are extracted directly from plants.

Many beginning soapmakers are surprised at the amount of essential oil required to give handmade soap a noticeable scent. The strong alkaline nature of the soapmaking process combined with their natural volatility means that you need to add enough essential oil so the smell is still detectable in the finished soap.

Remember, essential oils are incredibly powerful substances that shouldn't be handled carelessly. When working with them, always wear gloves to avoid getting undiluted oil on your skin. If you're pregnant, nursing or have certain medical conditions, check with your health care provider before handling them, as some essential oils may be contraindicated for you.

Below, I've listed several essential oils that you can use alone or incorporated as part of a blend. Amounts given are suggestions only, based on general guidelines for safe usage rates and influenced by my personal experiences and preferences.

ESSENTIAL OILS CHARACTERISTICS

BASIL (*OCIMUM BASILICUM CT. LINALOOL*)—a stimulating spicy sweet aroma that blends well with peppermint or lavender. Its use in select anti-aging and acne products make it a great candidate for use in facial soaps. Basil has an intense smell that can easily overpower other oils in a blend, so less is best with this oil. Use up to 10 grams in the recipes in this book, which contain 28 ounces (794 g) of carrier oils.

BERGAMOT (*CITRUS BERGAMIA*)—a sweet uplifting citrus-like scent that blends well with lavender, rosemary, orange, lemongrass, litsea and patchouli. Use up to 30 grams in the recipes in this book, which contain 28 ounces (794 g) of carrier oils. Avoid using old or oxidized oils to reduce risk of skin sensitization.

CEDARWOOD ATLAS (*CEDRUS ATLANTICA*)—an earthy woodsy aroma that blends well with lavender, patchouli, cypress, fir needle, eucalyptus and vetiver. Its astringent and antiseptic properties make it an excellent addition to facial or shaving soaps. While appreciated by both men and women, the scent tends to be a favorite for use in men's grooming products. Use up to 30 grams in the recipes in this book, which contain 28 ounces (794 g) of carrier oils.

CINNAMON LEAF (*CINNAMOMUM ZEYLANICUM*)—a deliciously warm and spicy fragrance that blends well with clove, patchouli, orange, lavender and fir needle. Cinnamon essential oil is very strong and can be a skin irritant when used in large amounts. Consult with a health care provider before use if you are pregnant, nursing, on medication or before using on a young child. Cinnamon essential oil can also speed up trace, making your soap thicken too fast to work with, so lightly hand stir into soap batter just before pouring it into a prepared mold. Use up to 6 grams in the recipes in this book, which contain 28 ounces (794 g) of carrier oils.

CLARY SAGE (*SALVIA SCLAREA*)—a lovely calming floral scent that blends well with lavender, geranium, listea (may chang), grapefruit and cedarwood. Its popular use in formulas for hair loss and dandruff makes it a good addition to shampoo bar recipes. If pregnant or nursing, check with a health care provider before use. Use up to 25 grams in the recipes in this book, which contain 28 ounces (794 g) of carrier oils.

CLOVE (*SYZYGIUM AROMATICUM*)—a strong spicy scent that blends well with cinnamon, ginger, orange, patchouli, cedarwood and fir needle. Clove oil is quite strong and should be used sparingly as an accent scent. Consult with a health care provider before use if your are pregnant, nursing, on medication or before using on a young child. It can speed up trace, making your soap thicken up too fast to work with, so lightly hand stir it in just before pouring soap into a prepared mold. Use up to 6 grams in the recipes in this book, which contain 28 ounces (794 g) of carrier oils.

COFFEE (*COFFEA ARABICA*)—smells like a freshly brewed cup of coffee and is perfect for adding scent to coffee soaps, such as Mocha Coffee Bean Scrub Bar, page 140. Use up to 25 grams in the recipes in this book, which contain 28 ounces (794 g) of carrier oils.

CYPRESS (*CUPRESSUS SEMPERVIRENS*)—a gentle oil with a clean evergreen scent that blends well with cedarwood, lavender, patchouli, clove, fir needle and vetiver. It has astringent properties and is helpful for balancing oily skin. Use up to 30 grams in the recipes in this book, which contain 28 ounces (794 g) of carrier oils.

EUCALYPTUS (*EUCALYPTUS GLOBULUS*)—a strong, cooling camphor-like scent that blends well with peppermint, lavender, fir needle and rosemary. Consult with a health care provider or trained aromatherapist before using on children under age 10. Use up to 25 grams in the recipes in this book, which contain 28 ounces (794 g) of carrier oils.

FIR NEEDLE (*ABIES SIBIRICA*), ALSO CALLED SIBERIAN FIR—a fresh clean scent that's reminiscent of walking through a pine grove. It blends well with cedarwood, eucalyptus, rosemary, vetiver, cypress and clove. Use up to 30 grams in the recipes in this book, which contain 28 ounces (794 g) of carrier oils.

GERANIUM (*PELARGONIUM GRAVEOLENS*)—a lovely mood-lifting rose-like scent that blends well with lavender, litsea, bergamot, orange and clary sage. Geranium is useful for both dry and oily skin conditions so goes well in all types of soaps. Use up to 25 grams in the recipes in this book, which contain 28 ounces (794 g) of carrier oils.

GRAPEFRUIT (*CITRUS × PARADISI*)—a clean happy fresh aroma that blends well with other citrus oils such as orange, lemon, lime, bergamot, along with litsea, lemongrass and lavender. By itself in a soap, grapefruit doesn't always hold its scent well; try anchoring it with some litsea essential oil or including it as part of a blend for best results. Grapefruit essential oil is useful for toning oily skin. Use up to 40 grams in the recipes in this book, which contain 28 ounces (794 g) of carrier oils.

JUNIPER BERRY (*JUNIPERUS COMMUNIS*)—has a warm woodsy fragrance that blends well with orange, fir needle, cypress, cedarwood Atlas and lavender. It may be helpful for problematic skin conditions and oily hair. Use up to 25 grams in the recipes in this book, which contain 28 ounces (794 g) of carrier oils and yield 2.5 pounds (1.13 kg) of soap.

LAVENDER (*LAVANDULA ANGUSTIFOLIA*)—has a calming herbaceous floral scent that blends well with almost all essential oils. Lavender is a gentle and well tolerated essential oil that's useful for many skin conditions, while the aroma helps calm nerves and relieve stress. Use up to 35 grams in the recipes in this book, which contain 28 ounces (794 g) of carrier oils.

LEMON (*CITRUS LIMON*)—has a fresh clean citrus fragrance that blends well with orange, litsea, lime, grapefruit, cedarwood and rosemary. Its astringent properties help to tone oily skin and hair. Regular lemon essential oil will not survive the saponification process well, so look for stronger folded versions labeled 5× (five-fold) or 10× (ten-fold) or use lemongrass essential oil for a longer lasting lemon-like scent. Use up to 40 grams in the recipes in this book, which contain 28 ounces (794 g) of carrier oils.

LEMONGRASS (*CYMBOPOGON CITRATUS*)—has a lemony aroma that blends well with orange, grapefruit, litsea, lavender, cedarwood and rosemary. Its ability to repel insects makes it a great choice for outdoor soaps. It also helps give soap a lemon-like scent that sticks around in soap longer than regular lemon essential oil does. Consult with a health care provider before use if you are pregnant, nursing or on medication. Avoid use on children under age 2. Use up to 20 grams in the recipes in this book, which contain 28 ounces (794 g) of carrier oils.

LIME (*CITRUS AURANTIFOLIA*)—has a strong citrus fruity scent that blends well with lemon, lemongrass, bergamot, grapefruit, litsea, patchouli, lavender and clary sage. As with the other citrus essential oils, the astringency of lime helps cleanse and tone oily skin and hair. By itself in a soap, lime doesn't always hold its scent well; try anchoring it with some litsea or lemongrass essential oil or including it as part of a blend for best results. Avoid using old or oxidized oils to reduce sensitization. Use up to 40 grams in the recipes in this book, which contain 28 ounces (794 g) of carrier oils.

LITSEA (*LITSEA CUBEBA*)—also called may chang. Has a lovely lemon-like scent that blends with citrus essential oils equally as well as florals. Try blending it with orange, grapefruit, lemongrass, lavender, geranium or rosemary. It acts as a useful anchor note when combined with more fleeting citrus scents such as grapefruit, lime, lemon and orange. It's often used for those with skin problems, though a small subset of the population may be prone to sensitivity to it. Consult with a health care provider before use if you are on medication. Avoid use on children under 2. Use up to 22 grams in the recipes in this book, which contain 28 ounces (794 g) of carrier oils.

ORANGE, SWEET (*CITRUS × SINENSIS*)—a fresh cheerful citrus scent that blends well with grapefruit, lemon, lemongrass, litsea, cinnamon, clove, patchouli and lavender. Orange essential oil brightens and tones all skin types. The fragrance of regular orange essential oil doesn't survive the soapmaking process well, so look for folded types such as 5× (five-fold) or 10× (ten-fold) orange. Orange Valencia (*Citrus × sinensis 'Valencia'*) also holds its scent well in soap. Use up to 40 grams in the recipes in this book, which contain 28 ounces (794 g) of carrier oils.

PALMAROSA (*CYMBOPOGON MARTINII*)—a somewhat rose-like scent and blends well with geranium to mimic a rose fragrance, or you could try it with orange, lavender, bergamot, litsea and clary sage. Palmarosa offers a host of benefits for all skin types. Use up to 20 grams in the recipes in this book, which contain 28 ounces (794 g) of carrier oils.

PATCHOULI (*POGOSTEMON CABLIN*)—a warm exotic aroma that blends well with most essential oils and offers a host of skincare benefits. When used in small amounts, it can anchor and subtly improve the scent profile of many blends, even for those who aren't normally patchouli fans. Use up to 30 grams in the recipes in this book, which contain 28 ounces (794 g) of carrier oils.

PEPPERMINT (*MENTHA × PIPERITA*)—a strong fresh minty scent that blends well with spearmint, lavender, lemon, basil, rosemary, eucalyptus, fir needle and tea tree. When coupled with clay, peppermint makes a lovely cooling soap perfect for washing up after a hot summer day. Avoid use on young children and those with cardiac fibrillation or G6PD deficiency. Use up to 25 grams in the recipes in this book, which contain 28 ounces (794 g) of carrier oils.

PERU BALSAM (*MYROXYLON BALSAMUM*)—a rich and sweet balsamic vanilla scent. It's used in small amounts as a base or anchor note in blends. Peru balsam can act as a sensitizer for some people, so use sparingly in blends. Avoid use on children under 2 and those with sensitive skin. Use up to 10 grams in the recipes in this book, which contain 28 ounces (794 g) of carrier oils.

ROSEMARY (*ROSMARINUS OFFICINALIS*)—a strong herbal scent that blends well with peppermint, lavender, tea tree, bergamot, lemongrass and litsea. Its scalp-stimulating properties make it especially fantastic for use in shampoo bars to promote hair growth and fight flakiness. Avoid use on young children. Consult with a health care provider before use if your are pregnant or have epilepsy. Use up to 20 grams in the recipes in this book, which contain 28 ounces (794 g) of carrier oils.

SPEARMINT (*MENTHA SPICATA*)—a sweet minty fragrance that blends well with peppermint, lavender, rosemary and basil. Like peppermint, it cools and soothes, but in a subtler gentle way. Use up to 25 grams in the recipes in this book, which contain 28 ounces (794 g) of carrier oils.

TEA TREE (*MELALEUCA ALTERNIFOLIA*)—a strong resinous scent that blends well with peppermint, rosemary, lavender and clary sage. It's often used for its powerful disinfectant and antimicrobial properties. Use up to 25 grams in the recipes in this book, which contain 28 ounces (794 g) of carrier oils.

VETIVER (*VETIVERIA ZIZANIOIDES*)—a relaxing earthy aroma. When you first smell vetiver out of the bottle it will seem overpowering, but it's wonderful for using in small amounts as a base or anchor note in blends. Vetiver is known for its positive effect on nervousness and depression. Use up to 15 grams in the recipes in this book, which contain 28 ounces (794 g) of carrier oils.

YLANG YLANG (*CANANGA ODORATA*)—a heavy sweet floral scent that blends well with orange, grapefruit, bergamot, lemon, geranium and lavender. It's used to calm nerves and balance all skin types. Avoid use on children under 2. Consult with a health care provider before using if you have low blood pressure. Used in small amounts, it acts to enhance essential oil blends. Use up to 15 grams in the recipes in this book, which contain 28 ounces (794 g) of carrier oils.

HOW TO BLEND ESSENTIAL OILS

Many soapmakers find themselves interested in creating their own essential oil blends, but aren't quite sure where to start. In this section, I'll share some basic tips and guidelines which can be used as a starting point.

Some essential oils, such as lavender, peppermint, litsea and lemongrass can be used alone in soap and still hold their desired scent for a long time. Other essential oils, such as orange, lemon, lime and grapefruit, are more fleeting and do best when paired with complementary oils whose scents are deeper or longer lasting.

When building a blend, you should generally aim for a mixture of top, middle and base notes, or at least a combination of a top note with either a middle or base note.

A top note is the scent you detect when you first smell a blend. Examples of top notes are anise, basil, bergamot, clary sage, eucalyptus, grapefruit, juniper (can also act as a middle note), lavender (can also act as a middle note), lemon, lime, orange, peppermint, pine, spearmint and tea tree.

A middle note is kind of like the bridge between top and base notes. It first mingles with the lighter top note in a blend, but the scent sticks around even after the top note fades, so it blends into the heavier base note as well. Examples of middle notes are bay, cinnamon, clove, cypress, elemi, fir needle, geranium, ginger (also acts as a base note), juniper (can also act as a top note), lavender (can also act as a top note), lemongrass, litsea, palmarosa, rose, rosemary and ylang ylang (can also act as a base note).

A base note is the scent that you don't detect at first because your brain is busy enjoying the top and middle notes, but it sticks around the longest and gives depth to the blend. Some base notes such as patchouli and vetiver have a heavier scent when used alone, so some people are turned off by them. When combined with other essential oils though, they really shine. Examples are cedarwood, ginger (also acts as a middle note), oakmoss, patchouli, peru balsam, sandalwood, vanilla, vetiver and ylang ylang (can also act as a middle note).

Some essential oils straddle the line between two categories, so you might find them listed differently, depending on who is compiling the list. An example of this is lavender. It's an instantly recognizable scent that can be detected right away in a blend, so is sometimes listed as a top note. However, it's more enduring than your typical top note and does well forming the heart of a blend, making it more of a middle note.

There's no set-in-stone rule about how much of each type of note you should use in a blend. Generally, the top and middle notes make up the larger portion of a blend, with the heavier base notes comprising a smaller amount. Don't be afraid to experiment with creative essential oil combinations!

Since the heat and high alkalinity of the saponification process can alter how some essential oils smell in the finished soap, it's always a good idea to try a blend idea out in a small test batch of soap first.

These sample blends and combinations are sized for the recipes in this book which contain 28 ounces (794 g) of carrier oils and yield 2.5 pounds (1.13 kg) of soap.

SIMPLE COMBINATIONS

LAVENDER LITSEA
0.70 oz (20 g) lavender essential oil

0.53 oz (15 g) litsea essential oil

LAVENDER TEA TREE
0.70 oz (20 g) lavender essential oil

0.28 oz (8 g) tea tree essential oil

DOUBLE MINT
0.53 oz (15 g) peppermint essential oil

0.53 oz (15 g) spearmint essential oil

ROSEMARY MINT
0.53 oz (15 g) peppermint essential oil

0.35 oz (10 g) rosemary essential oil

ORANGE SPICE
1.06 oz (30 g) 10× or Valencia orange essential oil

0.18 oz (5 g) cinnamon leaf essential oil

GRAPEFRUIT DELIGHT
1.06 oz (30 g) grapefruit essential oil

0.35 oz (10 g) litsea essential oil

JUNIPER ORANGE
1.06 oz (30 g) 10× or Valencia orange essential oil

0.28 oz (8 g) juniper essential oil

MELLOW CEDAR
0.78 oz (22 g) cedarwood Atlas essential oil

0.63 oz (18 g) lavender essential oil

BLENDS

LAVENDER ROSE GARDEN

0.70 oz (20 g) lavender essential oil

0.28 oz (8 g) geranium essential oil

0.14 oz (4 g) palmarosa essential oil

REFRESHINGLY CLEAN

0.56 oz (16 g) peppermint essential oil

0.28 oz (8 g) eucalyptus essential oil

0.14 oz (4 g) tea tree essential oil

LEMONY MINT

0.42 oz (12 g) lemongrass essential oil

0.28 oz (8 g) 10× or Valencia orange essential oil

0.21 oz (6 g) lime essential oil

0.21 oz (6 g) spearmint essential oil

ORANGE PATCHOULI

0.56 oz (16 g) patchouli essential oil

0.28 oz (8 g) 10× or Valencia orange essential oil

0.28 oz (8 g) lavender essential oil

CITRUS SPICE

0.88 oz (25 g) 10× or Valencia orange essential oil

0.28 oz (8 g) litsea essential oil

0.14 oz (4 g) patchouli essential oil

0.14 oz (4 g) clove essential oil

SUMMER NIGHTS

0.88 oz (25 g) 10× or Valencia orange essential oil

0.42 oz (12 g) grapefruit essential oil

0.21 oz (6 g) patchouli essential oil

0.14 oz (4 g) ylang ylang essential oil

CALMING FLORAL

0.85 oz (24 g) lavender essential oil

0.21 oz (6 g) litsea essential oil

0.14 oz (4 g) clary sage essential oil

SPICED COFFEE

0.70 oz (20 g) coffee essential oil

0.14 oz (4 g) clove essential oil

0.14 oz (4 g) cinnamon leaf essential oil

FOREST MINT

0.56 oz (16 g) peppermint essential oil

0.35 oz (10 g) fir needle essential oil

0.14 oz (4 g) rosemary essential oil

WALK IN THE WOODS

0.99 oz (28 g) cedarwood Atlas essential oil

0.14 oz (4 g) clove essential oil

0.14 oz (4 g) vetiver essential oil

LAVENDER HERB GARDEN

0.70 oz (20 g) lavender essential oil

0.35 oz (10 g) bergamot essential oil

0.14 oz (4 g) rosemary essential oil

CITRUS FOREST

0.56 oz (16 g) 10× or Valencia orange essential oil

0.42 oz (12 g) cedarwood Atlas essential oil

0.14 oz (4 g) 5× lemon essential oil

0.14 oz (4 g) vetiver essential oil

OTHER NATURAL SOAP INGREDIENTS & ADDITIVES

Besides natural colorants and essential oils, there are other ingredients you can use to add visual interest, texture and label appeal to your soaps.

AGAVE (*AGAVE TEQUILANA*)—a natural sweetener produced from agave plants. It's used in small amounts in soap as a vegan alternative to honey and to add label appeal. While it doesn't have the same nutritional benefits as honey, the natural sugars in agave help add a small boost to soap's lather. Add up to 1½ teaspoons (7.5 ml) to the 2.5 pound (1.13 kg) recipes in this book.

ALOE VERA LIQUID (*ALOE BARBADENSIS*)—a thin water-like liquid derived from aloe. It can be used to replace part or all the water in a recipe. Soaps made with aloe are extra bubbly and moisturizing.

BEE POLLEN—rich in protein, amino acids and antioxidant flavonoids; it can be ground into a fine powder and added directly to soap recipes. (See Bee Pollen & Honey Soap, page 113). Use up to 2 teaspoons (5 g) in the 2.5 pound (1.13 kg) recipes in this book.

BEESWAX—a wax secreted by worker honeybees. Used in small amounts (between 0.5 to 3 percent), it hardens soap and reduces the risk of soda ash (see page 184) from developing.

BLUEBERRY SEEDS (*VACCINIUM CORYMBOSUM*)—adds gentle exfoliation and a speckled appearance in soap. Use up to 2 teaspoons (6 g) in the 2.5 pound (1.13 kg) recipes in this book.

COFFEE GROUNDS (*COFFEA ARABICA*)—provides texture, exfoliation and visual interest in soap. Used grounds are generally recommended as less scratchy and less likely to bleed color into the surrounding soap. You could also use very fine espresso-style powder for lighter exfoliation. Use up to 2 teaspoons (3 g) in the 2.5 pound (1.13 kg) recipes in this book.

CORNMEAL (*ZEA MAYS*)—used as a mild exfoliant to polish skin. Use up to 1½ teaspoons (5 g) in the 2.5 pound (1.13 kg) recipes in this book.

CRANBERRY SEEDS (*VACCINIUM MACROCARPON*)—similar to blueberry seeds, they add gentle exfoliation and visual interest to soap. Use up to 2 teaspoons (5 g) in the 2.5 pound (1.13 kg) recipes in this book.

HONEY—a humectant, attracts moisture to skin and helps soften rough, aged or damaged complexions. The natural sugars in honey help to promote a better lather in soap. Use up to 2 teaspoons (10 ml) in the 2.5 pound (1.13 kg) recipes in this book.

JUNIPER BERRIES (*JUNIPERUS COMMUNIS*)—a main flavoring agent in gin, juniper berries are stimulating and antiseptic. They can be ground up and added to the lye solution (see Zesty Juniper Berry & Orange Soap, page 119) and used as a decorative topping for soap. Try adding up to 2 teaspoons (2 g) of ground juniper berries to the lye solution in the 2.5 pound (1.13 kg) recipes in this book.

OATS (*AVENA SATIVA*)—soothes itchy irritated skin and acts as a mild exfoliant. Make sure to grind the oats to a fine powder before adding to soap so they won't be scratchy. Use up to 1 tablespoon (7 g) of ground oats in the 2.5 pound (1.13 kg) recipes in this book.

POPPY SEEDS (*PAPAVER SOMNIFERUM*)—gives an attractive speckled look and exfoliating properties to soap. Use up to 1 teaspoon (3 g) in the 2.5 pound (1.13 kg) recipes in this book.

ROSEHIPS (*ROSA* SPP.)—the fruit of roses. High in flavonoids, they can be simmered with water for around an hour, then cooled to create a tea that can be used to make lye solutions. (See Wild Rosehips & Honey Soap, page 114.)

TUSSAH SILK—gives a luxurious silky feel to soap and boosts lather. Add a tiny pinch of silk fibers to the hot lye solution of any recipe and stir well.

USING HERBAL INFUSIONS TO ENRICH SOAP RECIPES

The world around us is filled with plants that contain compounds that can soothe, soften and nourish our skin. In traditional herbalism, those plants are steeped or infused in oil or water in order to best extract the beneficial properties in a way that's easy to apply directly to our skin.

While there's no doubt that these herbal preparations can be used in soapmaking as well, the big question is whether any of the benefits survive the high alkalinity and heat of the soapmaking process. There's no clear-cut answer to this question, due to the lack of scientific trials, but there's evidence to support that many herbal compounds that have been studied individually could make it through the soapmaking process because of their resistance to high temperatures and alkaline environments. It's also backed by years of my personal experience and the experience of other veteran soapmakers I've talked to—there is a noticeable difference in soaps made with certain herbs and soaps made without.

Whether or not the benefits of plants and plant extracts truly survive the soapmaking process, it's still fun to include them in recipes as part of the creative process and for added label appeal. In this section, we'll cover all the details of how to incorporate herbs into oil, water and milk infusions for your soaps.

SUGGESTED HERBS FOR INFUSIONS

CALENDULA FLOWER (*CALENDULA OFFICINALIS*)—helps regenerate damaged or broken skin; good for all skin types.

CHAMOMILE FLOWER (*MATRICARIA CHAMOMILLA*)—calms and soothes itchy or inflamed skin and scalp.

COMFREY LEAF AND ROOT (*SYMPHYTUM OFFICINALE*)—soothes irritated skin and scalp.

DANDELION (*TARAXACUM OFFICINALE*)—the flowers are soothing to chapped, dry, cracked skin while the leaves and roots may be useful for acne-prone skin.

ELDER FLOWERS (*SAMBUCUS NIGRA*)—an old-fashioned remedy for clear and beautiful skin.

FORSYTHIA FLOWERS (*FORSYTHIA SUSPENSA*)—a common bright yellow flower that can add a subtle golden tint to soap along with label appeal.

GOLDENROD FLOWERS (*SOLIDAGO* SPP.)—fall-blooming and used externally in herbal medicine for treating aches and pains; adds a subtle yellow color to soap.

HELICHRYSUM (*HELICHRYSUM ARENARIUM*)—also known as immortelle, the flowers and essential oil are used for their anti-aging properties.

HORSETAIL (*EQUISETUM ARVENSE*)—high in silica; strengthens and nourishes hair.

LAVENDER (*LAVANDULA ANGUSTIFOLIA*)—anti-inflammatory, calms and soothes skin.

MYRRH (*COMMIPHORA MYRRHA*)—useful for damaged or aged skin.

NETTLE (*URTICA DIOICA*)—highly nutritive; encourages strong and healthy hair growth.

PLANTAIN (*PLANTAGO MAJOR*)—a common leafy green weed; relieves itchy skin and scalp; soothes and restores damaged skin.

ROSE PETALS (*ROSA* SPP.)—a classic skin-soothing anti-inflammatory favorite for incorporating in natural beauty and body care recipes.

ROSEMARY (*ROSMARINUS OFFICINALIS*)—antiseptic and astringent; popular in shampoo bars for its ability to increase scalp circulation and encourage new hair growth.

SUNFLOWER (*HELIANTHUS ANNUUS*)—skin-soothing and conditioning.

YARROW (*ACHILLEA MILLEFOLIUM*)—tightens and tones oily skin and scalp.

PREPARING HERBAL OIL INFUSIONS

There are three basic methods of incorporating herbs into an oil you can use in your soap recipes:

THE QUICK METHOD

This method works especially well if you're the type of soapmaker who enjoys coming up with spur-of-the-moment soap ideas. You can be struck by a brilliant recipe idea, make the needed infused oil and have it turned into soap within a matter of hours. This method is also preferred for coconut oil, since it becomes too solid at cooler room temperatures to infuse as well.

Fill a heatproof jar around one-half full with your chosen herb or flower, or combine several herbs at once. Fill the jar almost to the top with your chosen oil. For soapmaking, this tends to be olive or coconut oil.

Set the uncovered jar down into a saucepan containing several inches of water, forming a makeshift double boiler. Place the pan over low heat for two to three hours. Keep a close eye during this process to ensure that the water doesn't evaporate. After the oil has infused to your satisfaction, remove the jar from the pan and set aside until it's cool enough to handle. Strain the oil through a fine mesh sieve or cheesecloth. If you don't plan on using the oil right away, you can leave it unstrained for several more days or weeks so it can continue to infuse while awaiting use.

THE WARM SUNNY-WINDOW METHOD

This process uses the natural heat of sunlight to jump-start the infusion process. It's not as fast as the quick method, but still quicker to make than the slow traditional method.

Fill a canning jar about one-half full with your chosen herb or flower, or combine several herbs at once. Fill the jar almost to the top with your chosen oil; olive oil is a good choice, or if allergic, rice bran oil works well too.

Cover the top with a piece of cheesecloth or scrap of old t-shirt and secure in place with a rubber band. The breathable barrier ensures that no condensation builds up during the infusing time and keeps unwanted bugs and dust from falling in and contaminating the oil. Set the jar in a warm sunny window. Depending on the amount of sunlight and how hot the oil gets, your oil may be infused within three to five days. For a stronger oil, tuck the jar away in a dark cabinet and allow it to infuse for several more weeks. Short-term exposure to bright sunlight is okay, but over time will cause the herbal properties to degrade more quickly.

THE TRADITIONAL SLOW METHOD

This method takes the greatest amount of time and a good measure of patience, but the resulting infused oil will be beautiful and well worth the wait.

Fill a canning jar about one-half full with your chosen herb or flower, or combine several herbs at once. Fill the jar almost to the top with your chosen oil; olive oil is a good choice, or if allergic, rice bran oil works well too. Cover the top with a lid, label and tuck the jar away in a dark cabinet for four to six weeks, shaking occasionally as you remember. Once the oil is sufficiently infused, strain it through a fine mesh sieve or several layers of cheesecloth.

The estimated shelf life of infused oils is around 1 year, though that can vary depending on the quality of the oils you start with and how well it's stored. Keep infused oils in a cool dark area out of direct sunlight.

PREPARING HERBAL TEA INFUSIONS

Another way to include the nourishing benefits of herbs and flowers in your soaps are as water infusions or teas used in the place of plain distilled water.

For fresh whole flower heads or petals, such as dandelion, rose, calendula, chamomile, sunflower (petals only), elder flower, forsythia, goldenrod, honeysuckle, violet, lavender and hollyhock, fill a 1-quart (1-L) heatproof canning jar half-way with fresh flowers/petals. Heat distilled water until simmering. Pour the water into the jar and allow the flowers to steep for 20 minutes to an hour, keeping an eye that your tea (especially lavender) doesn't turn a too-dark color, leading to a brown soap. Strain and cool completely before using in a soap recipe.

The same flowers listed above, but in dried form instead of fresh, can be infused in a similar way, though you only need to fill the jar around one-fourth full of dried flowers/petals before proceeding.

For fresh herbal leaves and sprigs such as mint, lemon balm, basil, nettle, plantain, violet, sage and thyme, they can be roughly chopped before infusing to make measuring easier. Place around $1/2$ cup (about 8 to 15 g) of chopped herbs in a heatproof canning jar. Pour simmering hot distilled water into the jar. Infuse for anywhere from 5 to 45 minutes, then strain. Teas of this sort are easy to over-steep, turning your finished soap a medium to dark brown color, so you want a tea on the light-colored side. Cool completely before using in a soap recipe.

The same herbs listed above, but in dried form instead of fresh, can be infused in a similar way, though you'll only need $1/4$ cup (about 4 to 8 g) of dried herbs.

For finely powdered herbs such as chamomile, ginger, kelp, myrrh, nettle, parsley, rosemary, wheatgrass and yarrow, you will only need a small amount to make a concentrated tea. Start with 1 teaspoon per 1 cup (8 ounces) of distilled water and see how the color develops while it steeps. Many powdered herbs double as natural colorants, so check out the section on pages 145 to 154 to see the recommended amount for a particular herbal powder.

Once the tea has steeped to your satisfaction, strain and cool before using in your recipe. Warm tea can react adversely with lye and overheat, so cool the tea for several hours before using or if pressed for time, drop several ice cubes in the tea until it's cooler than room temperature.

You can store fresh herbal teas for up to 2 days in the refrigerator, or pour into ice trays, freeze until solid and store the resulting cubes in your freezer for 4 to 6 months.

PREPARING HERBAL MILK INFUSIONS

Because milk is heat-sensitive, herbal-infused milks are made in a different manner than water infusions or teas and take longer to prepare. Because of the extended infusing time, herbal flowers perform better than herbal greens such as mint, thyme, rosemary and lemon balm. The latter tends to turn soap shades of brown or orange-brown.

Place about $1/2$ cup (4 to 12 g) of flower petals such as calendula, rose, dandelion, chamomile, hollyhock, lavender, violet, sunflower, elder flower, forsythia, goldenrod and helichrysum in a heatproof canning jar. Pour 0.5 ounce (14 g) of simmering hot water over the flowers and let cool for about 5 minutes. This helps jumpstart the infusing process. Next, pour 8 to 10 ounces (227 to 283 g) of cold milk into the jar. Cover with a lid, label and place in the refrigerator to steep for 2 to 4 days. Strain, squeezing the milk from the flowers as you do so. Freeze in ice trays until solid, then store the infused milk cubes in freezer bags until ready to use, or for 4 to 6 months.

This method can be used with animal milks, such as goat and cow, or unsweetened and unflavored plant-based milks, such as coconut, almond and oat.

3 WAYS TO ADD MILK TO SOAP

The natural sugars in milk mean that it's prone to overheating or scorching. Because of this, when making a soap with milk, it's a good idea to work at cooler temperatures than you'd use for regular soaps made with distilled water. Be aware that a false trace (see page 182) is more common when working with low temperatures. While the fat content of milk varies among type, such as whole cow's milk, goat's milk, coconut milk and so forth, in general you don't need to adjust your recipe to account for that, other than making sure your superfat (see page 18) isn't too high to start with. Just know that milks higher in fat will likely make a creamier soap than low fat milks.

FREEZE THE MILK

For a full milk soap that replaces all or most of the water in a recipe with milk, you should make the lye solution with frozen or partially frozen milk. The easiest way to prepare for this is to weigh the amount of milk you need for the recipe directly into ice cube trays. Freeze until solid and store the cubes in freezer bags until you're ready to make soap. Remove from the freezer and place in a pitcher or deep mixing bowl when ready to make your soap. If you'd like, pour a small amount (0.5 ounce/14 g) of distilled water over the frozen milk, to give the dry lye a bit of liquid to start reacting with. As it meets the water, it will begin to heat up and melt the cubes of frozen milk.

Working slowly, sprinkle the lye about a tablespoon at a time directly over the frozen milk, stirring well after each addition. This process can take up to ten minutes to ensure that the lye is completely dissolved. Undissolved lye can cause problems in your final soap and make it unusable, so taking your time during this step is important. Using this method, the lye solution will stay cool and rarely go above 90°F (32°C). Combine the milk and lye solution with oils that have been warmed up to 100 to 110°F (38 to 43°C). For the lightest colored milk soaps, place the freshly poured soap in a refrigerator or freezer for 24 hours to prevent gel phase. (See page 21 for more on gel phase.) An example of a recipe made with a full amount of fresh milk is Classic Oatmeal, Milk & Honey Soap, page 80.

DILUTE THE MILK

Another method of adding milk, but without the need to freeze it first, is by using 50 percent distilled water to make the lye solution and 50 percent milk, added with the warmed oils. For example, if a recipe requires 10 ounces (284 g) of liquid, you would use 5 ounces (142 g) as distilled water to make the lye solution and 5 ounces (142 g) as milk (non-frozen) blended with the warmed oils, before adding the lye solution. An example of a recipe made with the milk into oils method is Coconut Milk Shampoo Sticks, page 98.

USE POWDERED MILK

A third method involves adding powdered milk to a soap recipe. A general guideline to keep in mind is to use 1/2 to 1 tablespoon (4 to 8 g) of dry milk powder for every 16 ounces (454 g) of oil/fat in a recipe, but feel free to experiment with this ratio to get the amount you like best. With this method, you weigh the milk powder and blend it thoroughly into the warmed oils before adding the lye solution. An example of a soap recipe with powdered milk added this way is Lavender Milk Bath Bars, page 79.

NATURAL SOAP TOPS

After freshly made soap is poured into a mold, there's a narrow window of opportunity for the soapmaker to manipulate the appearance of the top. In this section, I'll cover tips for making smooth tops, textured tops or decorating with botanicals and other natural ingredients.

SMOOTH TOPS

The easiest way to get a smooth top is to stir the soap batter just until light trace and then pour immediately into the soap mold. Gently bang the mold against the surface of your work area to release any trapped air bubbles and to smooth the top layer of soap. If soap was poured at a slightly thicker trace, you may need to smooth the top with a spatula. If your soap is consistently too thick to easily pour into a mold and you'd really like a smooth top, try adding an extra 0.5 ounce (14 g) of distilled water to the recipe, mixing at slightly cooler temperatures and hand stirring more than using the immersion blender.

TEXTURED TOPS

The trick to working with textured tops is to allow the freshly poured soap to sit in the mold for a short while, until it's thick enough to hold a peak. Depending on how thick the soap is when you poured it into the mold and whether it's a high olive oil soap, which sets up slowly, or a soap high in butters or tallow/lard, which sets up more quickly, this could take anywhere from 2 to 25 or more minutes. Common items you find hanging around your kitchen such as spoons, forks and spatulas can be used to create textures. There's no wrong way to texturize soap tops, so just enjoy the process. If you don't like how a design is turning out, you usually have time to smooth it back down with a spatula and try again a few times. Because the soap is still caustic at this point, be sure to wear gloves and goggles while texturizing the top of your soap.

BOTANICAL & NATURAL TOPPINGS

For added beauty, soaps can be topped with a variety of dried flowers and other natural toppings. It's important that whatever you add to soap tops is completely dry or it could potentially mold. Also, for practical purposes and ease of use, keep the amount of decorations on the light side.

Some examples of soap toppings that work well include calendula flowers and petals, coffee beans, cornflower petals, helichrysum flowers, juniper berries, lavender buds, oats, rose petals, coarse sea salt and sunflower petals.

Add the desired items to the top of your freshly poured soap carefully, lightly pressing into the soap batter while wearing gloves to help them stay on better. When cutting soaps that have toppings, lay the loaf of soap on its side before slicing into bars. This prevents small pieces of decoration from dislodging from the top and dragging across the soap, leaving grooves as it goes. Be aware that some botanical toppings will fade over time and with extended exposure to sunlight.

SIMPLE LAYERS

Layered soaps are fun to make and add visual interest to your soaps. There are two ways to approach layers; you can simply pour the different colors directly over each other, or break up each layer with a pencil line (see page 173). The first simple method is described here.

STEP 1

Have all the colorants you plan to use measured and ready to add directly to the soap batter, so you're not scrambling for them later.

TIP: To make it easier to clean the immersion blender between colors, run hot water in a deep container or bucket and place it in your sink. After mixing one color of soap, place the immersion blender in the hot water and run the motor for several seconds until clean or mostly clean. Rinse and then wipe off any remaining batter with a paper towel.

Measure and mix a batch of cold process soap and bring it just to a light trace. Divide the soap equally into two or three containers, depending on how many layers you want your soap to have. While you can eyeball that amount, it works best to add up the weight of the oil, lye and liquid in your recipe, then divide that by 2 or 3 to determine exactly one-half or one-third. All of the recipes in this book, except the shave soap on page 123, weigh 2.5 pounds (1.13 kg).

STEP 2

Take one of the containers of plain soap and stir in the bottom layer's colorant. Blend with an immersion blender until a medium thick trace is reached.

Carefully pour the soap into the bottom of the mold. Gently rap the mold against the table to release any trapped air bubbles. Use a spatula to smooth the top of the soap if you'd like even layers. Conversely, you can use a spoon and texturize the top if you'd like more textured uneven layers.

STEP 3

Add the second layer's colorant to a container of plain soap. The soap may start thickening at this point, but that's okay. Stir it a few times with a spatula to loosen it back up. Mix the soap to a medium trace and carefully pour the second layer. Pour close to the mold and over a spatula to help prevent the layers from breaking into each other. Rap the mold against the work surface a few times again to help release air bubbles and so the layers settle into each other.

STEP 4

Stir the final layer's colorant into the last container of plain soap batter and carefully pour into the mold, using the spatula trick from step 3 to keep the layers from breaking into each other. Gently rap the mold on the table to get rid of any air bubbles.

STEP 5

Cover and let the soap go through gel phase to encourage the natural colorants to show up more brightly. Remove from the mold and slice into bars.

PENCIL LINE

A pencil line is thin horizontal line that's used to divide layers of soap and add visual interest. While you can experiment with using different natural colorants to create the line, cocoa powder is an easy one to start with.

STEP 1

Gather the supplies you'll need. For this project, I used cocoa powder and a mesh teaspoon, but you can use a fine sieve as well.

STEP 2

Pour the first layer of your soap. Place a small amount of cocoa in the mesh teaspoon or sieve and lightly sprinkle over the surface. You want just a light layer of cocoa powder as too much could prevent the two layers of soap from sticking together.

STEP 3

Carefully pour the second layer of soap over the cocoa powder. Pouring close to the mold and over a spatula helps reduce the risk of the top layer breaking through the bottom layer.

STEP 4

Cover and insulate for 24 hours before unmolding. When cutting soap with pencil lines, be sure to turn the loaf on its side, so the cocoa powder doesn't smear across the soap.

TIGER STRIPE

The tiger stripe technique, created by Kenna Cote of Modern Soapmaking, is one of the simplest ways to add visual interest to your soaps. Its forgiving nature makes it a great choice for your first attempt at creating a soap design.

STEP 1

Have all the colorants you plan to use measured and ready to add directly to the soap batter, so you're not scrambling for them later.

Measure and mix a batch of cold process soap and bring it just to a very light trace. For an easier time making designs and swirls in soap, increase the water amount of the recipes in this book to 9 ounces (255 g) and do not over-mix with an immersion blender. Divide the soap equally into two containers. While you can eyeball that amount, it works best to add up the weight of the oil, lye and liquid in your recipe, then divide that by 2 to determine exactly one-half. All of the recipes in this book, except the shave soap on page 123, weigh approximately 2.5 pounds (1.13 kg).

Take one of the containers of plain soap and stir in the prepared colorant. Blend lightly with an immersion blender just until the color is incorporated. You can leave the other container of soap plain, for a white stripe, or color it with a complementary colorant.

STEP 2

Choose a color to start with and pour a single stripe of soap batter down the center of the mold. Pick up the other container of soap batter and pour a stripe of batter directly over the first stripe. Then repeat with the first color. Keep alternating colors and pouring single stripes down the middle of the mold. Don't pour from too low or the colors won't break through each other. Instead, hold the containers up and away from the top of the mold for greater effect. Continue alternating stripes of color until the mold is filled.

STEP 3

Scrape any remaining batter from the containers onto the top of the mold. The top will look messy at this point. Use a knife, spatula or wooden skewer to lightly drag a zig zag (as shown), figure 8 or looping design over the batter, neatening up the appearance. Cover and allow the soap to go through gel phase, so the natural colorants show more brightly.

IN THE POT SWIRL

This technique is a simple way to produce a lovely swirl design in your soap, without a lot of fuss. Make sure your batter isn't too thin, or your colors will muddy together.

STEP 1

Have all the colorants you plan to use measured and ready to add directly to the soap batter, so you're not scrambling for them later.

Measure and mix a batch of cold process soap and bring it just to a very light trace. For an easier time making designs and swirls in soap, increase the water amount of the recipes in this book to 9 ounces (255 g) and do not over-mix with an immersion blender. If making a two-colored swirl, weigh 16 ounces (454 g) of soap batter into a separate container. If making a three-colored swirl, weigh 8 ounces (227 g) of soap batter into a small container and another 8 ounces (227 g) of soap batter into a separate container.

Mix the soap colorants into the smaller containers of batter, as desired, blending with an immersion blender just until the color is mixed completely. You don't want the soap to thicken too much or it won't pour or swirl well.

STEP 2

For a two-colored swirl, take the smaller container of colored soap batter and, holding it fairly high (about 2.5 ft/0.76 m) above the larger container of plain batter, pour one-fourth of it in one spot. Choose a spot opposite the area you just poured into and pour another one-fourth of the batter. Choose a spot between those two areas and pour another one-fourth, then pour the final amount of colored soap batter opposite that spot.

For a three-colored swirl, take one of the small containers of colored soap batter and, holding it fairly high (about 2.5 ft/0.76 m) above the larger container of plain batter, pour half of it all into one spot. Choose a spot opposite the area you just poured into and pour the rest. Do the same thing with the second container of color, choosing two different spots to pour into. Do not stir the soap at any time during this process.

STEP 3

Using a spatula, stir through the soap batter once or twice, but no more than that or you could muddy your colors together. Make sure your spatula hits all the way to the bottom of the container of soap batter so all of it is slightly swirled.

STEP 4

Without further stirring, carefully pour the soap batter into and across the soap mold until filled. Scrape any remaining batter from the individual containers in lines over the top of the soap. The top will look messy at this point. Use a knife, spatula or wooden skewer to lightly drag a zigzag (as shown), figure 8 or looping design over the batter, neatening up the appearance. Cover and insulate to allow the soap to go through gel phase, so the natural colorants show more brightly.

FUNNEL POUR

In this technique, alternating colors of soap batter are poured through a funnel, creating a beautiful design. While not necessary, you may want to enlist a friend's help to hold the funnel while you pour, after providing them with goggles and a pair of gloves.

STEP 1

Have all the colorants you plan to use measured and ready to add directly to the soap batter, so you're not scrambling for them later.

Measure and mix a batch of cold process soap and bring it just to a light trace. Divide the soap equally among three or more containers. While you can estimate that amount, it works best to add up the weight of the oil, lye and liquid in your recipe, then divide that by 3, or however many colors you want to use, to get the weight you need for each portion. All of the recipes in this book, except the shave soap on page 123, weigh approximately 2.5 pounds (1.13 kg).

Take one of the containers of plain soap and stir in a prepared colorant. Blend with an immersion blender just until blended, taking care that your soap batter doesn't thicken up too much in the process. If it becomes too thick, it won't pour through the funnel well. If that happens, you may want to try the tiger stripe design instead. Color the other container(s) of soap as desired.

STEP 2

Position the funnel over the center of the mold, where it will stay throughout the entire process. Pour just a small amount of the first color through the funnel, into the mold. Place that container down, then pour a small amount of another color through the funnel. Keep alternating colors until all of the soap batter is used. To ensure fairly even layers, try counting the same number of seconds (around 3 or 4) for each pour.

STEP 3

Smooth or texturize the top, as desired. Cover and insulate to allow the soap to go through gel phase, so the natural colorants show more brightly.

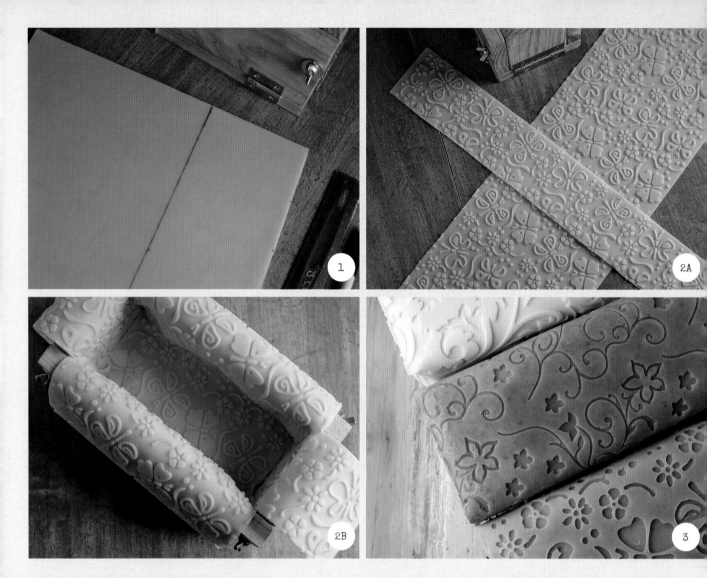

IMPRESSION MATS

Impression mats are an easy way to add beautiful artistic designs to the outside edges of your soaps.

Found in the cake decorating section of most craft stores or online (see the resource section at the end of this book), impression mats were initially designed for creating intricate detail on fondant. Here, we're going to cut an impression mat to create a textured liner for a loaf soap mold that can be reused over and over. As a bonus, you can flip the liner over so the smooth side is against the soap, for those times when you don't want a design imprinted on the surface.

STEP 1

Assemble the supplies you'll need: fondant mat, ruler, permanent marker, scissors and your soap mold.

Lay the fondant mat across the length of your mold, positioning it so it's taller rather than wider. Use a ruler to measure out the width of the mold from the margin of the fondant mat, starting at the top and working your way to the bottom, marking the spots with small dots. Connect the dots to form a straight line. Cut along the line. You should end up with a long skinny piece of fondant mat that fits neatly inside your mold and extends over the sides.

STEP 2

With the remaining large piece of fondant mat, do the same thing as before, only using the measurement for the length of the soap mold, making this piece larger. Press that piece inside the mold, over the long skinny piece.

STEP 3

To use, mix up a batch of soap to trace. Pour the soap batter into a mold lined with the cut pieces of impression mat. Keep the soap in the mold for 1 to 2 days. The impression mat should easily peel away from the sides of the soap loaf, leaving behind a clearly defined design.

SOAP STAMPS

Soap stamps are a simple way to decorate and personalize otherwise plain bars of soap.

Depending on the type of soap you're working with, it may be ready to stamp anywhere from a few hours after slicing into bars to a few days later. Harder soaps with lots of butters, tallow, lard or coconut oil will be ready to stamp sooner than castile soaps or those made with high amounts of olive oil. To avoid accidentally stamping too early on soap that isn't ready, cut a thin slice off the end of a loaf of soap you want to stamp and use that as a canvas for test stamping. If the first attempt results in the soap sticking to the stamp, you'll know to wait several hours or a day longer before trying again. Practice stamping on scraps and ends of soap every chance you get and you'll soon be a pro!

STEP 1

Choose a soap stamp and make sure it's completely free of any leftover soap bits. If necessary, use an old toothbrush to scrub out any hard to get spots.

STEP 2

Place the stamp on the bar of soap and firmly press into the surface, being sure that all four corners are pressed evenly. If you own a rubber mallet, you can lightly tamp the handle of the stamp to assist in this step.

STEP 3

Carefully lift the stamp off the surface of the soap and admire your work!

Part 4

Troubleshooting

Sometimes, soap just doesn't behave as it should. In this section, I've listed some of the most common issues that soapmakers run into along with a brief explanation and some tips to fix or avoid the problem next time.

Alien brains

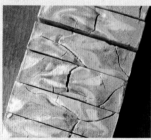

Crack develops on top of soap

Crumbling soap

COMMON SOAPMAKING ISSUES

ALIEN BRAINS—This creatively named soap condition is evident when soap overheats and leaves a wrinkled or brain-like look on the top. This is a purely cosmetic issue and your soap is still fine to use. To prevent this from happening again, mix soap at cooler temperatures and be careful to monitor freshly poured soap for signs of overheating.

CRACK DEVELOPS ON TOP OF SOAP—If you notice a crack developing along the top of your soap, it means that it's overheating and needs to be cooled down. Uncover the soap, if it was insulated, and move it to a cooler area or in front of a fan. If the soap stays covered and continues to overheat, it can develop into a soap volcano. Small cracks can be carefully pushed back together, but remember that the soap is still caustic and hot at this time, so wearing gloves is a must. Soaps high in honey, milk or other natural sugars tend to heat up more than soaps without these ingredients.

CRUMBLING SOAP—One common reason for soap to crumble is that it contains too much lye. Double-check the recipe with a lye calculator (see page 11) to be sure it has been calculated correctly. Sometimes, when measuring out oils, you may inadvertently leave one out, upsetting the lye to oil ratio. Keep a small list nearby and check off each ingredient as you add it, so nothing gets omitted. Soap can also become crumbly in spots when false trace happens. False trace is when cold temperatures cause solid fats (like butters) to start hardening before they've had time to come in contact with lye, leaving some parts of the soap lye heavy and others still oily. Separation may also occur with false trace. Soap that hasn't gone through gel phase can sometimes crumble more easily, especially when trying to cut it too soon after removing from the refrigerator or freezer. To reduce the chance of that happening, let the soap stay in the mold a few days longer after it has spent time in the refrigerator or freezer.

Dark spots in honey soaps

Glycerin rivers

Oil or glycerin oozing out

Partial gel

Separation or tunneling

DARK SPOTS IN HONEY SOAPS—If honey isn't thoroughly stirred into the soap batter, it can pool together in various areas of the soap, often near the bottom of the mold. These pools of honey can darken or scorch from the heat of gel phase, leaving behind oozing brown spots when you cut the soap into bars. This is a completely harmless condition, though unattractive for gift giving. To prevent this from happening in the future, dilute the honey with an equal amount of distilled water and be certain that it's thoroughly stirred into the soap batter before pouring into the mold.

GLYCERIN RIVERS—These are caused when the glycerin in the soap overheats and forms clear veins or marbling throughout the soap. Glycerin rivers aren't harmful and the soap is still great to use. In fact, most people who aren't soapmakers wouldn't realize that the design wasn't created intentionally. To reduce the occurrence of glycerin rivers in your soaps, work at lower temperatures and try reducing the amount of water in your recipe.

OIL OR GLYCERIN OOZING OUT OF SOAP—This is sometimes caused by humid weather or using tap water, which may contain unwanted minerals or contaminants, instead of distilled water. If it's just a small amount, visible as weeping droplets or a thin sheen, give the soap more cure time in the open air and it may reabsorb into the soap. You can lightly dab at the droplets with a paper towel or run a fan over the soap to speed up the drying process. If there's a visible puddle of liquid on top of the mold, or liquid gushes out when you cut a bar, the soap should be rebatched. (See page 185.)

PARTIAL GEL—This happens when the inside of your soap starts heating up during gel phase, but starts cooling off before the entire soap gels. As a result, the inside of the soap is usually darker than the outside edges. The soap is still fine to use. To prevent a partial gel, you can either force a full gel by working at warmer temperatures and heavily insulating the filled mold, or prevent gel phase by soaping at cooler temperatures and putting in the refrigerator or freezer for 24 hours after pouring. If you're plagued by partial gel when using loaf molds, try using individual molds instead, as they tend to cool down more evenly. If you notice a partial gel has formed in freshly made soap, you can sometimes save the appearance by carefully sliding it back into the mold and placing it in an oven turned on lowest heat for 1 hour.

SEPARATION OR TUNNELING—If your soap starts to separate in the mold, it may not have reached a full trace. Sometimes a false trace happens where the soap looks like it has emulsified, but it's only because a solid ingredient in the soap has gotten cool enough to start thickening the soap batter. Depending on the texture and workable nature of the separation, you could pour it back into your mixing container and stir/blend until a true trace is reached, or scoop into a slow cooker to hot process (see page 22). To make sure you're at a true trace next time, mix the soap until it appears trace has been reached, then let the soap batter sit for about 30 to 45 seconds. If the soap thins back out or has a visible oily layer, it's not at true trace and needs to be mixed further. If your loaf of finished soap looks fine on the outside, but has visible separate layers or tunnels containing liquid or oil throughout when cut into bars, it's likely caused by incomplete mixing. In this case, it's best to discard the soap, since portions will be lye-heavy.

Soap volcano

Soda ash

Soft soap

Soap stuck in mold

SOAP VOLCANO—This scary situation is when a soap overheats to the point of expanding out of a crack that develops across the top of the mold. To reduce the chance of this happening, keep a close eye on your soap in the hours after pouring. If it starts to develop a crack, move it to a cooler area, in front of a fan and/or elevate it on a cooling rack. If soap expands out of the mold and onto your work area, remember that it's still caustic and very hot. Wearing gloves and goggles, work carefully and use a spatula to scoop up the soap overflow. You can either place it in another mold and try to salvage it that way, or scoop it into a crockpot to rebatch (see page 185).

SODA ASH—This is a powdery white layer that develops over the soap. It's formed when the lye in the fresh soap batter reacts with carbon dioxide in the air. To prevent it, cover the soap after pouring into the mold with a layer of freezer or wax paper. Some soapmakers use plastic wrap instead or spray isopropyl alcohol over the surface of the soap. Soaping at higher temperatures, reducing the amount of water in your recipe and using distilled instead of tap water may also help reduce the chance of it developing. Soda ash is harmless, but if you don't care for the appearance you can steam it off with a handheld steamer or gently rub it off with a damp cloth.

SOFT SOAP—Squishy soft soap that feels like playdough can be caused by several reasons. First, double check your bottle of lye. If you shake it and hear clumps rattling around inside, it has collected moisture and won't measure out correctly. This leads to a soap that has too much oil for the amount of lye in it. You can still use this soap, though it will probably stay soft and oily. Another cause of soft soap is using too much water in your recipe. Let the soap cure in an area with good air circulation for several weeks and check it again. It may have just needed extra cure time. Soaps high in olive oil or other liquid oils tend to start off softer than those with lots of hard oils such as palm, tallow or lard. Try curing high olive oil soaps for several weeks or even months longer than other soaps.

SOAP STUCK IN MOLD—Some types of molds release soap better than others. Wooden molds should be lined with parchment or freezer paper to ensure an easy release. Many silicone molds, especially individual ones, release quite easily. Sometimes though, especially with deep square or rectangular molds, the soap gets airlocked and stays soft on the bottom. If your soap won't release from the mold after 2 to 3 days, you could either give it more time or place it in the freezer for 6 to 8 hours, until solid. Once frozen, the soap should push out easily. It's normal for the freshly unmolded soap to build up condensation while returning to room temperature, so I usually unmold frozen soaps onto a clean dishtowel or paper towel to absorb the moisture. Clear plastic molds are infamous for being difficult to unmold. When using them, reduce the water amount in the recipe and consider adding sodium lactate, a natural salt derived from the sugars in beets or corn, to produce a harder bar of soap. Even then, your soap may have to spend several weeks in a clear plastic mold until it contracts enough to release. You can also try refrigerating or freezing the mold for around 30 minutes to an hour, but be careful with freezing too long as it may cause the plastic to crack.

White spots on top of soap

WHITE SPOTS ON TOP OF SOAP—Sometimes, smooth flat white spots can appear on top of soap. While it's somewhat of a mystery as to why, it's often associated with soaps made with lavender essential oil. Most lavender soaps will not develop the white spots, but if they appear on yours, you'll know they're purely cosmetic and the soap is still usable. If the spots are sparkly or powder-like, however, they're more likely to be specks of undissolved lye and the soap should not be used.

HOW TO REBATCH OR SAVE A SOAP

If your soapmaking goes awry, there's no need to worry as some soapy mishaps can still be saved. If your soap is freshly poured and you notice it separating in the mold, or realized immediately after pouring that you forgot an oil, you can pour it right back into your mixing container, use an immersion blender to mix in the missing ingredient, mix to a true trace and then pour back into a mold. Once the soap begins to set up but is still actively saponifying, an immersion blender won't easily be able to mix it. For this situation, you would scoop the entire batch into a slow cooker, adding any missing ingredients if necessary, then hot process. (See page 22 for how to hot process soap.) Sometimes, you may need to rebatch a soap that's over 24 hours old and completely hardened. Maybe it didn't turn out exactly as you planned or you realized much too late that you forgot an oil or a key ingredient.

STEP 1

Grate or break the soap into small pieces and add them to a slow cooker. Add a few teaspoons of distilled water. If you're rebatching because you forgot an oil in the recipe, add the missing oil now.

STEP 2

Cover the crockpot and let the soap pieces cook on low heat, stirring occasionally. Add small amounts of water, 0.5 ounces (14 g) at a time, as needed, to prevent the soap from drying out. Continue cooking and stirring until the soap is a uniformly melted thick gloppy-looking mixture. This may take anywhere from an hour to several hours.

STEP 3

Remove the crockpot from the heat and spoon the hot soap into a mold, pressing to remove air pockets.

STEP 4

Allow the soap to cool in the mold, then slice into bars.

CONFETTI SOAP

If you find yourself with a batch that didn't quite turn out the color you wanted or have lots of odd-sized end pieces sitting around, don't throw them away! Instead, grate them up and make confetti soap.

STEP 1

Shred the unwanted soap pieces with a box grater or vegetable peeler.

STEP 2

Make a batch of Basic Palm-Free Soap, on page 38.

STEP 3

Bring the soap to a medium-thick trace, then fold the soap shreds into the batter.

STEP 4

Carefully pour the soap into a prepared mold. Cover, gel, unmold, slice and cure the soap as normal, then enjoy your new repurposed soap!

Resources

While some oils, herbs and other soapmaking additives can be sourced locally from grocery or health food stores, you can also find a wide variety of high quality ingredients and supplies by shopping directly from online soap suppliers. Below I've listed the websites for suppliers that I recommend in the U.S. and internationally.

SOAPMAKING SUPPLIES

UNITED STATES
Bramble Berry – www.brambleberry.com
Bulk Apothecary – www.bulkapothecary.com
Essential Depot – www.essentialdepot.com
Essential Wholesale & Labs –
    www.essentialwholesale.com
From Nature with Love – www.fromnaturewithlove.com
Lotioncrafter – www.lotioncrafter.com
Mad Oils – www.madoils.com
Majestic Mountain Sage – www.thesage.com
Mountain Rose Herbs – www.mountainroseherbs.com
Nature's Garden – www.naturesgardencandles.com
New Directions Aromatics –
    www.newdirectionsaromatics.com
Rustic Escentuals – www.rusticescentuals.com
Soap Goods – www.soapgoods.com
Soap Making Resource – www.soap-making-resource.com
Soaper's Choice – www.soaperschoice.com
Sweet Cakes – www.sweetcakes.com
The Chemistry Store – www.chemistrystore.com
The Herbarie – www.theherbarie.com
The Lye Guy – www.thelyeguy.com
Wholesale Supplies Plus –
    www.wholesalesuppliesplus.com

AUSTRALIA/NEW ZEALAND
Aussie Soap Supplies – www.aussiesoapsupplies.com.au
Escentials of Australia – www.escentialsofaustralia.com
Go Native – www.gonative.co.nz
Heirloom Body Care – www.heirloombodycare.com.au
New Directions – www.newdirections.com.au
Robyn's Soap House – www.robynsoaphouse.net
Sydney Essential Oil Company – www.seoc.com.au

CANADA
Aquarius Aromatherapy & Soap Supplies –
    www.aquariusaroma-soap.com
Canwax Candle & Soap – www.canwax.com
Candora Soap – www.candorasoap.ca
Cranberry Lane – www.cranberrylane.com

Creations from Eden – www.creationsfromeden.com
New Directions Aromatics –
    www.newdirectionsaromatics.ca
Saffire Blue – www.saffireblue.ca
Soap & More – www.soapandmore.com
Voyageur Soap & Candle –
    www.voyageursoapandcandle.com
Windy Point – www.windypointsoap.com

UK & EUROPE
Aroma Zone – www.aroma-zone.com
Aromantic – www.aromantic.co.uk
Cosmetics Natural Home Shop – www.cremas-caseras.es
Fresholi – www.fresholi.co.uk
Gracefruit – www.gracefruit.com
New Directions – www.newdirectionsuk.com
Organic Makers – www.organicmakers.se
Soapmakers Store – www.soapmakers-store.com

SOAP CUTTERS & STAMPS
Bud's Woodshop – www.etsy.com/shop/budhaffner
Custom Soap Stamps –
    www.etsy.com/shop/CustomSoapStamps
For Crafts Sake – www.forcraftssake.com
MRK-Tools – www.seifenschneider-mrk-tools.com
Nurture Soap – www.nurturesoap.com

HELPFUL WEB SITES
About Candle & Soap – www.candleandsoap.about.com
Great Cakes Soapworks –
    www.greatcakessoapworks.com/handmade-soap-blog
Humble Bee & Me – www.humblebeeandme.com
Lovin Soap – www.lovinsoap.com
Modern Soapmaking – www.modernsoapmaking.com
Soap Deli News – www.soapdelinews.com
Soap Queen – www.soapqueen.com
The Nerdy Farm Wife – www.thenerdyfarmwife.com
Natural Suds N More – www.naturalsudsnmore.com/blog

LYE CALCULATORS
Bramble Berry –
    www.brambleberry.com/pages/lye-calculator.aspx
Majestic Mountain Sage –
    www.thesage.com/calcs/LyeCalc.html
SoapCalc – www.soapcalc.net/calc/soapcalcwp.asp
Summerbee Meadow – www.summerbeemeadow.com/
    content/lye-calculator-and-recipe-resizer

About the Author

Jan Berry is a writer, herbalist, soapmaker and owner of the website The Nerdy Farm Wife. She lives on a small farm in the Blue Ridge Mountains of Virginia with her husband and two teenagers, along with a menagerie of animals. She enjoys gardening, reading, tabletop games and spending time with her family.

Acknowledgments

Thank you to readers of The Nerdy Farm Wife blog. Your continual support and encouragement touches me in so many positive ways. I'm thankful for you!

Thank you to Will Kiester and his amazing Page Street team for the opportunity and honor to write a second book; along with an extra special thanks to my editor, Sarah Monroe.

Much love and appreciation goes to my wonderful husband, who tirelessly and cheerfully helped make test batch after test batch of soap and supported me in every way possible during the writing process.

I want to also extend a very special thank you to my natural soapmaking group on Facebook who uplifts and inspires me each day; especially the following beta testers who spent their valuable time and ingredients making each recipe, offering feedback and ensuring every project in this book was adjusted until it was just right. Amy Sowers, Andrea Satterthwaite, Bélla Maria Fanucchi, Beth Sandahl, Betsy Fairfield, Chandice McInerney, Donna Morris, Donna Rader Ebert, Ellen Black, Ing Reils, Jeana Johnson, Jenna Hill, Jessica Devers, Jolene Etter, Kathy Campbell, Kathy Scalzo, Krasimira Peneva, Megan Swaney-Williams, Melissa Coleman, Michelle David, Michelle McLain, Miha Morosini, Noemi Gonzalez, See Heok and Suzzannemarie Dunne.

To my niece, Brooke Jarman, goes huge thanks for the help with several soapmaking batches and for her sweet spirit and creative input.

I'm truly grateful for my friend and master gardener, Kay Taylor, for providing some of the flowers for this book and for saving the day with a supply of rosehips after the local wildlife decided to eat all mine!

Thank you to Erin Stewart, Certified Aromatherapist and editor of *Aroma Culture* magazine, for reading through the essential oils section and offering valuable input.

Last, but certainly not least, I'd like to express my deepest gratitude to three early soapmakers who generously shared their hard-earned knowledge through their books, articles and websites and played a large part in my soapmaking journey—Sandy Maine, Susan Miller Cavitch and Kathy Miller (of millersoap.com).

Index